Encounter Jesus!

Encounter Jesus!

Transforming Catholic Culture in Crisis

PETER M. DOANE

WIPF & STOCK · Eugene, Oregon

ENCOUNTER JESUS!
Transforming Catholic Culture in Crisis

Wipf & Stock
An Imprint of Wipf and Stock Publishers
199 W. 8th Ave., Suite 3
Eugene, OR 97401

www.wipfandstock.com

PAPERBACK ISBN: 978-1-5326-9558-2
HARDCOVER ISBN: 978-1-5326-9559-9
EBOOK ISBN: 978-1-5326-9560-5

Manufactured in the U.S.A.   04/18/19

To my father, Edward, and my wife, Leslie.
They have served me and drawn me to Christ Jesus.

Contents

Preface

I Will Build My Church . . .

SACRED SCRIPTURE OFFERS US a picture of the church Jesus instituted. First, this sacred building would be built by Jesus Christ himself. It would not be built like the Old Testament Temple with stones chiseled in Solomon's quarries but rather as St. Peter told us, "like living stones, let yourselves be built into a spiritual house, to be a holy priesthood, to offer spiritual sacrifices acceptable to God through Jesus Christ" (1 Pet 2:5 NRSV, Catholic Edition). Secondly, this new presence in our time-space world would have a foundation described as "built upon the foundation of the apostles and prophets, with Christ Jesus himself as the cornerstone" (Eph 2:20). This new spiritual building would endure the test of time because of its foundation.

Historians inform us that this "building" seems to be severely tested every five hundred years. The first time the church was extremely tested was in the fall of Rome, the first five-hundred-year period. It had a rebirth when great missionary disciples like Augustine in England and Patrick in Ireland spread the faith and risked everything for the Name. Then came a second "earthquake" around the year 1000 with the Islamic invasions and the Great Schism of the church in Constantinople in 1054. All seemed lost, yet the Holy Spirit raised saints like Francis and Dominic, Clair and Catherine of Sienna.

In the third five-hundred-year period, nuns and priests were leaving their vocations. Tetzel was selling indulgences and then came the reformers who began reforming the faith, and there was nothing wrong with the faith—it was the moral culture that needed to be rebuilt. Teresa of Avila and John of the Cross arose and looked at and showed us what the actual building should be.

Throughout the history of the church, as it is continually being built, scaffolding surrounds its structure. Scaffolding is only used during the construction of a building; it does not support the building; the foundation does. Once the building is complete, the scaffolding is taken down. It may come as a surprise to some of us that the building continues to stand after the Lord removes the scaffolding. Sometimes it is hard for us to remember that the building is beautiful and eternal because of her Builder. The scaffolding that surrounds the building in every age, and every culture is a structure filled with materials and workers, both righteous and unrighteous. These are part of the necessary scaffolding, which will eventually be removed. Scaffolding surrounds the temple of the Lord, and now, after another five hundred years, the Lord is revealing the scaffolding. The Catholic Church, the Western church, finds itself in a deep crisis. The culture of the church has genuinely declined to the point that her integrity is questioned and even mocked. I wrote my book to address this crisis and offer answers that church history has shown will bring healing, restoration, transformation, and deliverance!

Our calling now becomes ever so clear. If we allow history to inform us, we, like Augustine in England and Patrick in Ireland, must focus on transforming the culture of the church, especially here in the West. Like St. Francis, we volunteer to become rebuilders and repairers. As Teresa of Avila and John of the Cross, we look through the scaffolding and rediscover its true spirituality. Jesus Christ continues to build his church in the context of human frailty and failure. May we, too, look at the building Jesus constructs and be ready to say, "yes" to the Master Builder! We must encounter Jesus Christ!

"Then I saw a new heaven and a new earth; for the first heaven and the first earth had passed away, and the sea was no more. And I saw the holy city, the new Jerusalem, coming down out of heaven from God, prepared as a bride adorned for her husband. And I heard a loud voice from the throne saying, "See, the home of God is among mortals. He will dwell with them; they will be his peoples, and God himself will be with them" (Rev 21:1–3).

P.M.D.

JULY 2019

CARMEL, INDIANA

Acknowledgments

I GRATEFULLY ACKNOWLEDGE THE research and contributions of Michelle P. Buckman, author and editor, and James P. Doane, MLIS. Their critical review of the entire manuscript and knowledge of proper writing format served me much in this process. I am indebted to St. Meinrad Seminary and School of Theology for helping me rediscover the Catholic faith after returning to the church. I am thankful to Father Ted Rothrock for taking a "risk" and hiring me as the director of evangelization after serving as a pastor and missionary in evangelical circles for over thirty years. I am grateful for Elisabeth Groot and John Shelton for trusting me and recommending me for ministry at St. Elizabeth Seton Catholic Church.

I acknowledge Wipf and Stock Publishers for accepting my manuscript and recognizing its message.

I am thankful for my four children, James, Benjamin, Joshua, and Abigail. They have supported Leslie and me as we searched and then found where the Lord was calling us.

I am grateful that Jesus brought my wife, Leslie, into my life. She has been a rock, a Proverbs 31 woman to our family and me.

Finally, and most importantly, I am thankful to Christ Jesus, who allowed me to encounter him powerfully and continues to lead me to reencounter him.

Introduction

As THE CHURCH THROUGHOUT *America prepared to commemorate the five hundredth anniversary of the first evangelization of the continent, when speaking to the Council of Latin American Bishops in Port-au-Prince (Haiti), I had said: "The commemoration of the five hundred years of evangelization will achieve its full meaning if it becomes a commitment by you the Bishops, together with your priests and people, a commitment not to a re-evangelization but to a new evangelization—new in ardor, methods, and expression.*[1]

There is a crisis of faith, and we are called to transform Catholic culture. The abuse crisis is the capstone for us losing our children, our influence, our institutions, our voice, and indeed, our Catholic identity.

What is needed for a transfromation? A *radical* response from all quarters of the Catholic Church in America. The word "radical" comes from the Latin word (1350–1400; Middle English < Late Latin) *rādīcālis* "having roots," equivalent to Latin *rādīc-* (stem of *rādīx*) "root" + *-ālis*.[2] For many, this book will seem radical, if not too extreme. The reason is, the roots of our faith, pictured for us in the Gospels and then lived out in the Acts of the Apostles, is most radical. It is the root system out of which we have been grafted in. In responding to the crisis, we will find Catholics taking different postures toward it. Some may become *defensive* and take the stance "to leave well enough alone and bury our heads in the sand." Others may become *hopeless* and adopt

1. Paul, *Apostolic Exhortation*, Intro 7.
2. "Radical," 1, https://www.dictionary.com/browse/radical.

a siege mentality. Others may say to *leave it in the hands of the Lord* and let him deal with it. Still others may return to previous responses regarding a need of renewal with *revolt and withdrawal.* Finally, some may *lose faith in God himself,* having put so much hope in having a perfect institution. *Encounter Jesus! Transforming Catholic Culture in Crisis* is a bold strategy drawing upon the roots of our faith. It is a call for us to revisit the Acts of the Apostles as the model for Catholic spirituality. It is a practical handbook explaining new initiatives to implement St. John Paul the Great's call for a new evangelization: *new in ardor, new in methods,* and *new in expression.* New in ardor means to recapture the zeal of the Apostolic age. "Ardor" comes from the Latin word *ard(ere),* to burn. In a culture of encounter, disciples begin to "burn" in their love for Jesus Christ and their compassion for lost and wandering people. New in methods means to recapture apostolic strategies and apply them to our twenty-first-century church. "Method" is a word derived from *meta + hodos,* meaning "way," or "road." The Latin *methodus* means a medical procedure. *Encounter Jesus!* will help us to restore the preaching of the *kerygma* in every Catholic seminary and parish and close the floodgates of Catholics leaving the church. New in expression means to step out of old ways of communicating our faith. The word "expression" comes from the Latin *expressio,* meaning "a pressing out." Transforming Catholic culture calls for us to "press out" of our predisposed patterns. We then "push in" to new modes: using classical education, music, art, drama, film, social media, and technology. We also "press in" to a primary focus of mission to evangelize and call clergy, consecrated religious, practicing Catholics, non-practicing Catholics, and non-believers to encounter Jesus Christ. If we *surrender* our wills to Jesus and offer ourselves on his altar of sacrifice, we will see the Lord do amazing works in the days, months, and years to come. Are you willing?

> I appeal to you, therefore, brethren, by the mercies of God, to present your bodies as a living sacrifice, holy and acceptable to God, which is your spiritual worship. Do not be conformed to this world but be transformed by

the renewal of your mind, that you may prove what is
the will of God, what is good and acceptable and perfect.
(Rom 12:1–2, NRSV, Catholic Edition)

Chapter 1

A Dramatic Story of Encounter

My father, a faithful and practicing Catholic, had an extraordinary encounter with Jesus Christ. His experience has become a
prophetic insight for me on what must take place in the lives of
individual Catholics. His story, atypical but universally applicable,
was first shared at his local parish, St. Michael's Catholic Church in
Newark, New York, during a planned cantata (a choral composi-
tion—sacred, secular, or resembling a short oratorio—as a lyric
drama set to music but not to be acted). In the presentation, there
called for a testimony by someone in the parish speaking in rela-
tion to the song "The Longer I Serve Him, the Sweeter He Grows,"
which was the final song in the "Alleluia, Let's Praise the Lord"
cantata.[1]

The following is a transcription from the tape recording that
evening:

> Good evening my brothers and sisters in Christ. *I'd like
> to talk to you for a few short minutes about Jesus Christ.
> I'd like to tell you what he did for me, how he changed my
> life, and what he means to me, today.*

---

1. William J. Gaither, *The Longer I Serve Him*, https://www.musicnotes.
com/sheetmusic/mtd.asp?ppn=MN0056493.

For fifty years, I believed that I was the captain of my ship and that I was the master of my soul with everything I did. I had a wonderful childhood; I sought out the sweetest girl in town (she became my wife); the Depression in 1931 came along, and we weathered that in satisfactory shape. My family grew; I had a glorious life with five healthy, beautiful children. I had a job at Eastman Kodak Company that I obtained, and I worked hard to get several promotions; I had a better than fair job. In fifty years, I believed I had everything under control. Oh, I believed in God; and I knew about Jesus Christ. I knew that God had sent Jesus to this earth some two thousand years ago, and he lived and died for us; and then I believed he had lived and died and gone to heaven and was sharing his throne with his Father in heaven. But two thousand years was a long time ago, and Heaven was ninety million miles away, as far as I was concerned. At fifty years of age I knew something was missing. I knew there was something in life that I didn't have, and I started a search. At that particular time, Father McDonald was a brand-new pastor of this church, and I came to Fr. McDonald, had a few short talks with him. He gave me several weeks of instruction, and I became a member of St. Michael's church.

For thirteen years, I religiously sought the God I was missing. I got right into the church. I attended Mass regularly; I kept the law and did everything I could. The church was real good to me. It gave me many positions of honor; I have been through all the offices, I believe, from Cub Scout Master to treasurer of the church; and I don't believe there was a financial committee I haven't served. Through adult education courses, I learned much; through the Sacraments, through the Eucharist, and through the church offering me abundant opportunities to serve, I felt my Catholic faith was complete. *But still, there seemed to be something missing.*

This change in what I was missing had to come through a little different situation and circumstance, and that event happened on the night of January 15, 1972. The situation was that I had a massive heart attack and a severe attack of Parkinson's disease. Between the two, the

Lord and I took a deep travel into the Valley of Death. And I mean it was deep because at one point my spirit left my body and plunged into death. I had the honor and privilege of getting a peek at what many people hope to see. The curtains were opened wide, and I was enveloped in the eternal beauty of heaven. I saw the beautiful colors that I don't believe any artist has words to explain. I saw the Eternal Light that gave heaven its eternal light of no day or no night, and the biggest privilege was I heard the voice of the Lord, and he spoke to me saying, "I do not want lip service, I want heart service; don't be so self-reliant, rely on me; don't be so self-sustaining, lean on me." He said, "For your church, I want spirituality and spiritual fellowship." With that, my soul and spirit came back to earth with the same speed that they had ascended.

But, after that experience, things were never the same. I started reading some Scripture. It seems that I couldn't lay my Bible down. I couldn't leave it long enough to eat. I read everything I could get my hands on. My mind and my heart were like a gigantic blotter, absorbing every word and soaking it in and holding it in my heart. Now Bible scholars say there are over three thousand six hundred promises in the Bible, and I believe I have read every one of them. But there is one short quote that has come to make a real change in my life, and that quote is from John 15:5, which says, "Apart from me, you can do nothing." And that, I believe, is what has been missing in my life. I had been trying to do it all without the Lord.

What a change this has made. The Lord is with me, and I believe this if you are around where I am now, you will hear me singing a particular song and that song is, "The Longer I Serve Him, the Sweeter He Grows.

St. John Paul II said: If it is genuine, the personal encounter with the Lord will also bring a renewal of the church: as sisters and neighbors to each other, the particular churches of the continent will strengthen the bonds of cooperation and solidarity in order that the saving work of

Christ may continue in the history of America with ever greater effect. Open to the unity which comes from true communion with the Risen Lord, the particular churches, and all who belong to them, will discover through their own spiritual experience that "the encounter with the living Jesus Christ" is "the path to conversion, communion, and solidarity." To the extent that these goals are reached, there will emerge an ever-increasing dedication to the new evangelization of America.[2]

Of course, my father's experience was dramatic. However, the frame surrounding his encounter with the Lord has several important elements to consider. First, my father fit the definition of a "faithful Catholic." After entering the Catholic Church, he attended Mass regularly, including daily Mass. He habitually received the sacrament of the Eucharist. He was very active in church functions, ministries, and adult formation opportunities. Yet with all these dynamics, he had not personally encountered Jesus Christ. While his encounter was not typical, the fruit of his encounter is typical and becomes apparent in all encounters with our Lord.

First, there became an intense desire to read and digest sacred Scripture. A hunger for the written word is the barometer of real encounter and ongoing encounter with Jesus Christ. When the Lord met the two disciples on the road to Emmaus, he explained the Scriptures to them, saying to them they were foolish men and slow of heart (Luke 24:25)! After Jesus had opened their eyes through the breaking of the bread, they reflected on the fact that their hearts burned within them as he opened to them the Scriptures (Luke 24:32). St. Jerome told us that "ignorance of Scripture is ignorance of Christ."[3] So, the first fruit of encounter is a discovery or rediscovery of Scripture playing a central role in the life of the Catholic Christian.

Second, a personal encounter with Jesus Christ creates a boldness that overflows into a witness and testimony to others. My father not only gave his testimony at his local parish. He began to

2 John Paul, *Apostolic Exhortation*, intro 7.

3. Schaff, *History of the Christian Church*, 977.

share his faith everywhere he went. Some of those who listened were moved. Some others rejected the testimony. Shortly after my dad's heart attack, he became dehydrated and was moved to the hospital. While he was there, he began to share his story and encounter with other patients. To his amazement, even many who were terminally ill wanted nothing to do with Jesus Christ. He often referred to this: "Even on a deathbed, some will continue to resist inviting Jesus Christ to take complete control and surrender to him."

Third, a personal encounter with Jesus Christ results in a desire to be in spiritual fellowship with other Christians. This kind of fellowship not only includes social events and gatherings, but also bible studies, small groups, adult faith formation opportunities, and sharing with others what the Lord is doing in one's personal life. This is the kind of fellowship we see in the Gospels and the Acts of the Apostles. On the day of Pentecost, after three thousand received St. Peter's invitation (the *kerygma*, by the way), they devoted themselves to the Apostles' teachings, fellowship, the breaking of bread (Eucharist), and the prayers (personal and liturgical). This is the lifestyle that emerges after an encounter—we do not remain the same!

YOUR CHALLENGE

Go into your inner room and tell Jesus you want everything he has for you in your relationship with him. Call on him and he will answer! Raise your hands to him and even fall prostrate before him!

Chapter 2

Restoring the Lost Treasure

And He said to them, "Therefore every scribe who has been trained for the kingdom of heaven is like a householder who brings out of his treasure what is new and what is old."

Matt 13:52

To build a culture of encounter in the Catholic Church, particularly in the West, we must recover the lost treasure found in the apostolic church: the *kerygma*. The term *kerygma* is a Greek word meaning "proclamation." The Greek word (*kerusso*) means "herald," or one who proclaims. And thus, the *kerygma* is that which is proclaimed. As the Apostles began the work of preaching and proclaiming Christ, they proclaimed a message that was rather basic and simple. More extensive teaching or instruction (*didache*) would come later, after baptism. But the initial proclamation of Christ was simple and to the point. Unfortunately, this treasure of the apostolic church has been lost in many of the Catholic parishes in America and the West. Our Catholic culture, therefore, consists of many "cradle Catholics" who have never received the invitation to "repent and call upon the name of Jesus."

On Easter of 2014, my son invited my wife Leslie and me to attend the Easter morning service in his Christian community.

Grace Community Church is a megachurch in Noblesville, Indiana. The pastor gave a simple yet powerful proclamation—the *kerygma*. The theme of the talk was "Jesus Met Me." He spoke of the time when Jesus met him in the dorm as a young college student. After his testimony, a series of videos, fifteen seconds in length, showed several people, of all ages, stating where Jesus met them. Some included the state of their lives when they had this encounter: a drug addict, a wealthy business person, a stay-at-home mom, a single father, and a young adult. One could feel the impact of these testimonies filling the auditorium. At the end, the pastor gave an invitation. The call asked people to look under their seat, where they would find a sheet of paper with the words, "Jesus Met Me." The pastor stated that Jesus could meet someone right there, where they were now sitting. After a prayer, he asked all whom Jesus was now meeting to please stand up. All over the auditorium, people were standing up. Behind me was sitting a family of five: mother, father, and three children between the ages of ten and fifteen, it appeared. They were all standing, holding up their signs, "Jesus Met Me." The woman, visibly moved, was crying. At that moment, I had the distinct impression this was a Catholic family. They were all encountering the living God. They were responding to the *kerygma* presented in such a simple yet clear proclamation, with an invitation. This treasure is lost in our Catholic culture, and it is a treasure more precious than silver and gold.

God gives us the prototype of the *kerygma* in the Acts of the Apostles. The ancient Christian *kerygma* as summarized by Dodd from Peter's speeches in the New Testament Book of Acts was:

1. The Age of Fulfillment has dawned, the "latter days" foretold by the prophets.

2. This has taken place through the birth, life, ministry, death, and resurrection of Jesus Christ.

3. By the resurrection, Jesus has been exalted at the right hand of God as Messianic head of the new Israel.

4. The Holy Spirit in the church is the sign of Christ's present power and glory.

5. The Messianic Age will reach its consummation in the return of Christ.

6. An appeal is made for repentance with the offer of forgiveness, the Holy Spirit, and salvation.[1]

On the day of Pentecost, Peter stood up with the eleven and addressed the crowd. In this sermon, we see him target the audience, proclaim the scripture, take nothing for granted, be specific, and give an invitation. Let's take a moment to dissect these five elements in St. Peter's address.

First, he knew and targeted his audience. People had gathered for the great feast in Jerusalem, a tremendous heterogeneous group. Peter understood, under the guidance of the Holy Spirit, his message had to be universal, one to which everyone could relate. All present heard in their own language, their own context. Therefore, this proclamation took place, so all could hear, all could identify. The *kerygma* related to all who were present. I am sure that all who heard the message, including those who had just come from the upper room, leaned toward Jesus and felt a call to go deep with Him.

St. John Paul II instructed us clearly here:

> The Proclamation is the permanent priority of mission. The Church cannot elude Christ's explicit mandate, nor deprive men and women of the "Good News" about their being loved and saved by God. "Evangelization will always contain—as the foundation, center, and at the same time the summit of its dynamism—a clear proclamation that, in Jesus Christ . . . salvation is offered to all people, as a gift of God's grace and mercy." All forms of missionary activity are directed to this proclamation, which reveals and gives access to the mystery hidden for ages and made known in Christ (cf. Ephesians 3:3–9; Colossians 1:25–29), the mystery which lies at the heart of the Church's mission and life, as the hinge on which all evangelization turns.

1. Dodd, *The Apostolic Preaching*, 22.

In the complex reality of mission, initial proclamation has a central and irreplaceable role, since it introduces man "into the mystery of the love of God, who invites him to enter into a personal relationship with himself in Christ" and opens the way to conversion. Faith is born of preaching, and every ecclesial community draws its origin and life from the personal response of each believer to that preaching. Just as the whole economy of salvation has its center in Christ, so too all missionary activity is directed to the proclamation of his mystery.

The subject of proclamation is Christ who was crucified, died, and is risen: through him is accomplished our full and authentic liberation from evil, sin and death; through him God bestows "new life" that is divine and eternal. This is the "Good News" which changes man and his history, and which all peoples have a right to hear.[2]

So, bishops, priests, and deacons should target their audience. In the audience, every time they are in the pulpit, there is a percentage, sometimes very great, who need to hear the proclamation of Jesus Christ. A priest once said in my presence, "Oh, I don't need to put much prep time into my Christmas homily; no one is listening." Although his attitude doesn't speak for the church at large, it does serve as an example of where the Catholic culture could use improvement. When God brings people to the church, whether at Christmas and Easter, or funerals and weddings, the homilists in the church should consider their audience and target it.

Secondly, when Peter proclaimed Jesus Christ on the Day of Pentecost, he quoted sacred Scripture to open the minds and hearts of the people. The Book of Hebrews tells us that God's Word is sharper than any two-edged sword (Heb 4:12). In Peter's address, he uses the Scriptures in a prophetic sense. The people can tie the moment to the writings. In proclaiming the prophet Joel and the psalmist David, the Apostle powerfully demonstrates how ancient writings apply to the here and now! Therefore, there must be a renewal, from those who preach from the ambo, applying the sacred writings to the everyday

2. John Paul, *Encyclical Letter Redemptoris Missio*, ch. 5, para. 44.

life of those who gather for Mass. The same Holy Spirit who penned the words through his human instruments is today present to "cut to the heart" the listeners of the message (Acts 2:37).

Third, when Peter preached the *kerygma* on the Day of Pentecost, he was taking nothing for granted. He assumed that all the listeners needed to hear the message. Often, I hear homilies implying all present have encountered Jesus because of their baptism. In that assumption, the homilist is doing irreparable damage to many of the listeners. It causes those who have never decided to surrender to Jesus Christ to become "inoculated" without ever receiving the true dynamic of the Gospel. Many of those baptized as infants have never heard the call to put their faith in Jesus Christ and make a personal commitment to him. Just as the Day of Pentecost called the listeners to action, so today's homilist must call into action those who have yet to "activate" their faith. Dr. Ralph Martin, Catholic theologian and leader in the New Evangelization, states this in his compelling explanation of the decline of Catholicism in the West:

> These directories make clear that conversion can't be presumed among those who approach the sacraments but must be called forth. They further make clear that sacramental preparation can't simply be a matter of providing "information" but must involve "formation." Formation involves a conforming of one's life to the truth which one is hearing and to the person who is the foundation of these truths and to the community of those who live these truths. It requires from the catechists modeling discipleship into which they are leading those whom they catechize. It is not just "religious education" but an invitation to conversion and a life of discipleship. These documents also make clear that the baptismal catechumenate is a model for all catechesis, as it involves in its essence not just information but formation.[3]

Dr. Martin is referring to The General (GDC) and National Catechetical Directories (NCD) and their clarion call for a new

---

3. Martin, "The Post-Christendom Sacramental Crisis," 64.

catechesis that begins with proclamation and conversion. There is a growing acceptance and understanding in the church that many of her children have been catechized but never evangelized. If the church is to be renewed, clergy, religious, and laity must begin to accept this essential premise.

Fourth, on the Day of Pentecost, St. Peter was very particular with his audience. He made Jesus Christ the center point of the proclamation. We cannot call people, first, to the Church. Benedict XVI, while still a Cardinal, noted we must speak about the church less and speak more about God and Jesus Christ. "Today, even critical minds are becoming more clearly aware of the fact that the crisis of our time consists of the 'crisis of God,' the disappearance of God from the horizon of human history. Thus, the church's response can only be to speak *less and less* about herself and *more and more* about God, to witness to him, to be a doorway for him"[4]

I see this time and time again. Often the homily in many parishes will extol the benefits of "converting" to the church. In fact, in many if not most Catholics' minds, conversion is synonymous with becoming a Catholic. "Did John convert to Catholicism?" is a common question. On the day of Pentecost, St. Peter did not preach the church. He proclaimed the name that is above all names (Phil 2:9–10). If we are truly converted, we have responded to the proclamation and surrendered first to a Person. That act of surrender leads one to renew their baptismal vows, if already baptized, renew openness to the Holy Spirit, if already Confirmed, and receive the Eucharist with renewed passion and reverence. It all starts with Jesus Christ, and a total surrender, which is what the Apostle called for on the Day of Pentecost. When this surrender took place in the hearts of the three thousand, we find the commitment to the church and her disciplines became the natural by-product.

Finally, the Apostle Peter, filled with the Holy Spirit, completed the *kerygma* by giving an invitation and a challenge. The preaching brought the crowd to conviction. In their conviction, their hearts cried out: "Brethren, what shall we do?" (Acts 2:37). We know the *kerygma* is delivered when the listeners are convicted and begin to

4. Ratzinger, *The Legacy of John Paul*, 33.

ask how they can be saved (or reencounter Jesus if that is the case). Peter told them: "Repent and be baptized every one of you in the name of Jesus Christ for the forgiveness of your sins; and you shall receive the gift of the Holy Spirit" (Acts 2:38). Peter did not stop with this invitation. He went on to challenge them: "And he testified with many other words and exhorted them, saying, 'Save yourselves from this crooked generation'" (Acts 2:40). So, within the proclamation we also are confronted with a challenge. The culture surrounding the new Christians was utterly corrupt, and Peter admonished them to depart from it. The *kerygma* would be the bridge that allowed the new disciples to find a new culture where this initial encounter would be nurtured through the teachings of the Apostles, fellowship, breaking bread, and prayers (Acts 2:42). Catechesis, spiritual fellowship, the Eucharist, and prayer (both personal and liturgical) became the lifeline of what it meant to be disciples.

Jesus told St. Peter he would give him the "keys to the kingdom of heaven": "And I tell you, you are Peter, and on this rock, I will build my church, and the powers of death shall not prevail against it. I will give you the keys of the kingdom of heaven, and whatever you bind on earth shall be bound in heaven, and whatever you loose on earth shall be loosed in heaven" (Matt 16:18–19).

The *kerygma* delivered by Peter on Pentecost fulfilled the promise Jesus made to him. The "keys to the kingdom of heaven," which open the doors of the hearts of men and women, young and old, were taken out of the Apostle's heart by the Holy Spirit and unlocked the hearts of these first Christians. Nothing less will cause the church to be renewed and revitalized.

May the *kerygma* again find its place in the heart of the church so the keys to the kingdom of heaven can unlock the hearts of the people.

YOUR CHALLENGE

Study the content of the *kerygma* modeled by St. Peter in the Acts of the Apostles. Then, whether clergy, religious, or lay person, begin to look for the "open door" and proclaim it!

Chapter 3

Cradle Catholics and Encounter

MY WIFE AND I were "cradle Catholics." A cradle Catholic is not a recently baptized infant/child that sleeps in a cradle. This Catholic slang refers to someone baptized and raised Catholic that might go to Sunday Mass but may be somewhat indifferent to the faith. Indifferent in the sense that they do not understand Catholicism or have not learned more about their faith, their salvation, and eternal things. Leslie and I went to Sunday Mass with our families, but as we grew older, we were not sure how it applied to our lives. We were not sure *why* we were spending an hour a week at our parishes down the street. God was in this box, and the rest of our lives were outside the box. With this backdrop, both Leslie and I, separately, had life-changing encounters with Jesus. Our stories are more typical of what can happen in the life of Catholics, especially young adults. As young adults, we both were "lost" in our faith and the Lord came out and found us!

Leslie's story began in Pittsburgh, Pennsylvania, where she was born into a devout Italian Catholic family. Her earliest memories are of dresses prepared for Sunday Mass and school uniforms with starched white blouses set out for her and her sisters every weekday morning. She attended Catholic grammar school from kindergarten through the eighth grade. She vividly remembers every Christmas Eve. The family gathered with excitement in the family room and removed from the shelf the large family Catholic Bible to read the story of Christ's birth. Then the family recited the rosary. This formation in her domestic church included regular Mass attendance on Sundays and Holy Days of Obligation, Catholic grammar school, recitation of the rosary and Catholic prayers, first confession, first communion, teaching nuns, visiting priests, and May "crownings." She was immersed in a Catholic culture during her formative years. Adolescence encompassed the typical life of a Catholic teen: regular Mass attendance, high school friends from various Christian communities, and increased detachment from the daily expression of faith. A close friend with a Baptist background invited Leslie to a Young Life retreat. Young Life is a non-denominational Christian ministry that reaches out to adolescents through volunteers, staff, club meetings, and camps by building meaningful relationships with high school students. At the retreat she attended, the Christian college students who hosted the event shared the *kerygma*. For the first time in Leslie's life, she heard that Jesus Christ wanted to have a *personal relationship* with her. They went on to share how Jesus died and rose again so this could be possible. My wife heard something that weekend that she had never heard before. Her response was not an immediate one, but rather she stored away the experience. Later, in college, the Lord "followed up" with her at a campus prayer meeting. The seed that God had sowed in her was watered and began to grow. A full commitment to Jesus Christ followed as, again, the *kerygma* was spoken of and proclaimed among the college students.

The two of us met at this campus ministry and fellowship. Incidentally, we both concur, approximately 75 percent of the two hundred students came from a Catholic background. It was at this campus ministry that so many of them heard the *kerygma* for the first time, or in Leslie's case, had those seeds watered so that they could sprout.

My experience somewhat mirrors Leslie's. I was brought up in an Irish-American Catholic family. My earliest memories are of attending a weekly meeting in homes throughout the neighborhood to pray the rosary for the conversion of Russia. I too attended Sunday Mass with my parents and never missed a Holy Day of Obligation. I went to a Catholic grammar school, St. Michael's, in

Newark, New York. The Sisters of Mercy nuns were my teachers in all classes, kindergarten through eighth grade. I memorized the Baltimore Catechism, as all Catholic children did. When I was nine years old, I experienced a mystical revelation of Jesus Christ. My mother's habit was to pray for me each night in my bedroom, kiss me goodnight, and leave the room. One night, during our ritual, after she left the room, the Lord revealed himself to me. I saw Him hanging on the cross, but unlike any crucifix I had ever seen. He was naked and looked like a mangled animal and not a man. Only later was I to learn the Isaiah passage that states: "Just as there were many who were astonished at him—so marred was his appearance, beyond human semblance, and his form beyond that of mortals" (Isa 52:14). I wept and wept during those moments.

This encounter caused me to make an initial commitment to Jesus along with an initial repentance. I experienced a genuine conversion at that time. I carried this relationship in the privacy of my soul and do not remember any sources reinforcing this personal encounter.

There was another encounter, later, in seventh grade. I was an altar boy and was serving the Monday night novena at our church. That evening I had the censer and it was my role to incense the Eucharistic Jesus who was present in the ciborium. During the liturgy, the Lord visited me again. I was overwhelmed on that altar with the presence of God as we adored Jesus in the Eucharist.

Time passed as I made my way through public high school, attending Mass and going to CCD classes. But there was a definite slow but steady departure from who I had come to know. Finally, in my senior year of school, the Lord had become a distant figure in my life. I now headed toward a fractured existence modeling the journey of the Prodigal Son in Luke's Gospel.

I spent my first two-and-a-half years of college spiritually lost. My model for living reflected a 1960s St. Augustine. My sin produced loneliness, confusion, addictions, and depression, with complete separation from my Lord, but thanks be to God, the heavenly Father came out to meet me! He sent young men from Ohio State and the Campus Crusade for Christ. They preached the Gospel to me and others at Bowling Green State University in Ohio. When I heard the words of the *kerygma*, my heart burned and melted. When they left the house, I went up to my bedroom, got on my knees, and called out to the Lord. He swept into that room and drove the darkness from my being. I rediscovered the God of my childhood in power and deliverance. I could feel a stench leave me as I prayed to Jesus and called on his name.

The immediate result was dramatic. The following Monday, I attended my morning classes. My friend Harriet looked at me and said: "Peter, what's going on? You look so healthy!" I shared what had happened to me, and that initiated a series of experiences sharing it with those who knew me. I went to a party the following weekend where many of my friends were doing drugs. I sat down to talk with Marc, and he said this to me: "Peter, I am on a hallucinogen, and everything in this room is moving except one thing—your face!" I repeated to him what had happened to me. (For a complete story of my experience, my years as an evangelical Protestant pastor, and my return to the Catholic Church, see bibliography).[1]

Countless people had the same experience as Leslie and I during the Jesus Movement days of the late '60s and throughout the '70s.[2] As mentioned earlier, the Christian Fellowship at Bowling Green State University, which I helped found and lead, was filled with Catholic young adults who had responded to the preaching about Jesus Christ. The commitment made by these young people was dramatic. At the heart of the conversion stories was, again and again, the simple proclamation of the death, burial, and resurrection of Jesus Christ and the invitation to change your life by surrendering to him. It worked then just as it did on the Day of Pentecost. It works today. Our Catholic culture must be transformed to embrace this norm and practice it everywhere!

YOUR CHALLENGE

Catholic parents, in fulfilling your call to be the first educators of your children, share your faith story, regularly, with them. Bring them to a personal encounter with Jesus Christ!

1. Doane, "A 'Convoluted' Pathway Home."
2. "The Jesus Revolution."

Chapter 4

"Tolle lege! Tolle lege!"

To ENCOUNTER JESUS CHRIST and then to continually encounter him, Catholics should read, study, meditate, and fellowship with others over the sacred Scriptures. An emphasis on digesting the Scriptures will indeed be a seedbed for cultural change within the church. Although Catholics hear the Scriptures every time they attend Mass, there needs to be a revolution in personal and communal study of God's Word.[1] The well-known monk St. Jerome tells us that "ignorance of Scripture is ignorance of Christ."[2] The ignorance Jerome speaks of is not primarily an ignorance of intellect, but rather an ignorance of encounter, relationship, and dialogue with the living Christ that comes from the written Word of God.

Our beloved St. Augustine had his life forever changed when he encountered the Lord through sacred Scripture.[3] In Milan, Augustine came under the influence of Saint Ambrose, the bishop; he began to go to his sermons, not so much from a desire to convert but rather to satisfy his curiosity. He found that the talks and discussions were more compelling than the philosophies he had

---

1. Longenecker, "Why Don't Catholics Read the Bible?"

2. Schaff, *History of the Christian Church*, 977.

3. "Saint Augustine: Bishop of Hippo, Doctor of the Church (A.D. 430)." http://www.copticchurch.net/topics/synexarion/augustine.html.

embraced. The teachings of Ambrose led him to read the New Testament, especially Saint Paul's writings. During this period, the mother of his son, Adeodatus, went back to Africa, leaving the child behind with Augustine.

Saint Augustine's wrestling continued; he was becoming convinced of Christianity, but he still embraced the worldly temptations and therefore delayed his surrender to Jesus for many months. "Soon, in a little while, I shall make up my mind, but not right now," he kept telling himself. As he toyed with conversion, he would seek God for grace but was, at the same time, not yielded to the one calling him. He began to realize that his problem was doublemindedness. His conversion would never take place, unless, like the Blessed Mother, he said, "yes."

During this time, Pontitian, an African, came to visit Saint Augustine and his friend Alipius; he told them about two men who suddenly converted by reading about the life of Saint Anthony. Pontitian's words had a powerful impact on Saint Augustine. He was stirred yet he was weak and said to Alipius:

"What are we doing to let the unlearned seize Heaven by force, while we with all our knowledge remain behind, cowardly and heartless, wallowing in our sins? Because they have outstripped us and gone before, are we ashamed to follow them? Is it not more shameful not even to follow them?"

He ran into the garden, greatly upset; he threw himself on the grass under a fig tree and humbled himself and cried out:

"And Thou, O Lord, how long? How long? Is it to be tomorrow and tomorrow? Why not now? Why not this very hour put an end to shame?"

As he said this, he heard a child's voice singing, "Tolle lege! Tolle lege!" (Take up and read! Take up and read!). He could not remember this chant from his childhood. But, He recognized that Saint Anthony converted by hearing a single verse.

He took up Saint Paul's epistles and read the first chapter he saw:

"Let us walk honestly, as in the day; not in rioting and drunkenness, not in chambering and wantonness, not in strife and envying. But put ye on the Lord Jesus Christ, and make not provision for the flesh, fulfil the lusts thereof " (Romans 13:13–14).

When he told Alipius of his experience, Alipius took the book and read and found the next words to be: "Him that is weak in the faith receive ye," which he applied to himself and joined Augustine in a similar commitment.

This high point in the conversion of Saint Augustine took place in September of 386 when he was thirty-two years old. He, his son Adeodatus, and Alipius were baptized by St. Ambrose at Easter the following year in the presence of St. Monica. She knew her prayers were answered and died shortly after.

Saint Augustine prayed:

> Too late, have I loved Thee, O Beauty so ancient and so new, too late have I loved Thee! Thou wast with me, and I was not with Thee; I was abroad, running after those beauties which Thou hast made; those things which could have no being but in Thee kept me away from Thee. Thou hast called, Thou hast cried out, and hast pierced my deafness. Thou hast enlightened, Thou hast shone forth, and my blindness is dispelled. I have tasted Thee and am hungry of Thee. Thou hast touched me, and I am afire with the desire of thy embraces.[4]

St. Augustine's testimony is a powerful witness to the transformational place that reading the sacred Scriptures can play in your life and the life of your loved ones. St. Augustine's witness points to the benefits you will reap by doing this!

When my father passed on to his reward, I took his Bible into my possession. It remains a source of inspiration to me as I periodically peruse those worn pages.

Investing in reading Scripture is putting treasure into our "spiritual bank." As we build a reservoir within our daily reading, the Holy Spirit can brood (Gen 1:2) within our lives and bring the Scripture to the forefront for real-life application. The best example of this is found in the confrontation Jesus had with Satan

---

4. Schaff and Wace, *A Select Library*, 152–53.

in the wilderness. It was his use of the Scripture that defeated the devil's temptation.

Should we assume we can be successful in our spiritual warfare, as well as the entire human journey, without the word of God living deeply within us? I believe we need to follow St. Augustine's example.

These realities motivate one to look at priorities and set new goals. Someone once said: "If you aim at nothing, you'll be sure to hit it!" There are many dimensions we need to consider in our pursuit of spiritual growth and spiritual health. Most importantly, many do not consider that spiritual growth is based on God's permission! In the book of Hebrews, the writer states: "Therefore let us go on toward perfection, leaving behind the basic teaching about Christ, and not laying again the foundation: repentance from dead works and faith in God, instruction about baptisms, laying on of hands, resurrection of the dead, and eternal judgment. And we will do this *if God permits*" (Heb 6:1–3, emphasis added). Here, we see that our growth toward perfection (maturity) is, first of all, a grace gift from the Lord. If he permits, we can move toward perfection. My response to this reality is to humble myself, confess my inadequacies, and surrender to the Lord and his plan.

Once I take this posture, I can begin to set my goals. A goal I suggest is the discipline of reading scripture, starting in the New Testament, one chapter per day. This is foundational to all spiritual life in Jesus Christ. An easy yet efficient way to address this vital area is something I call Advance 260 because there are two hundred and sixty chapters in the New Testament. By reading one chapter, from Monday through Friday, it is possible to digest the entire New Testament in a year, all books in fifty-two weeks. Saturdays and Sundays are free. If a day in the week is missed, it can be recovered during the weekend.

Most chapters in the New Testament take from three to seven minutes to read, which is not a big portion of our day! One can incorporate this into morning devotions, during a meal, or at bedtime. Families can participate in reading during the meal, which is a good Benedictine discipline. I have decided to read my chapter during my work week lunch hour. There are several reading plans to choose from. The important thing is to choose one and begin to incorporate it into your lifestyle.

Why is reading the Scriptures so vital? St. Paul said the kingdom of God is not in word only but also in power (1 Cor 4:20). There is power in God's Word to transform us. When we read and digest the Scripture, it has the power to change us. Recent studies on the brain suggest that we can fill up crevices in our brain that addictions, evil thoughts, pornography, and doubts have created.[5] What a wonderful goal for our daily fellowship with God. We can change the way we think and be more in line with the way God thinks. "*Tolle lege! Tolle lege!*"

YOUR CHALLENGE

Make a commitment to read the sacred Scriptures every day. Choose a plan and stick to it. If you miss a day, or several days, don't give up! Reading Scripture will transform you!

5. Paredes, "Here's What Porn Addiction Does."

Chapter 5

The Elephant in the Room

DO YOU FEEL THAT members of your family or friend's receive their Sacraments but don't live them out? You're not alone. The Sacraments of Initiation are given with the correct "matter" and "form," but statistically, the church is losing adherents in droves. If people who have left the Catholic Church formed a denomination, it would be the second largest church body in America.[1]

In a previous chapter, we discovered the "lost treasure" of the church: the proclamation of the Gospel (*kerygma*). Directly tied to the lost treasure is the teaching or catechesis (Greek, *didache*) instructing Catholic people correctly about the reception of the Sacraments. Why is there such an attrition among Catholics who have received these Sacraments of Initiation (Baptism, Confirmation, and Eucharist) as well as the sacrament of Penance and the sacrament of Matrimony? Religious education instructors, catechists, and the Rite of Christian Initiation of Adults (RCIA) teams look for the "key" to unlock the graces the Sacraments speak of, theologically, but our experience teaches us something entirely different.

More Catholics are praying less, attending Mass infrequently, giving less, and adopting more of the pervasive secular culture.

1. Roberts, "The 'Had It' Catholics," para. 8.

Statistics show us the grim reality following teenage Confirmation classes. The majority leave the church, and connections with their faith cease. In RCIA classes, statistics point out that up to 50 percent of those received into the church lose their connections after two years. According to Sherry Weddell, her unscientific yet massive relationships with parishes around the United States surmise that a mere 5 percent of parishioners in any local congregation in America would fall into the category of a practicing disciple.[2]

What are we to name this elephant in the room? The teaching of St. Thomas Aquinas reveals the precise answer to that question: the receiver of any sacrament has a serious part to play in that sacrament bearing fruit in the life of the Catholic Christian! While the Sacraments play an irreplaceable role in the life of the church, large percentages of the faithful are not only not benefiting from the sacramental life, they are finding the liturgies annoying, without any real-life application.

The response to the Protestant Reformation was one that began to emphasize strongly *ex opera operato* (by the fact of the action being performed) in the Sacraments and deemphasized the importance of *ex opera operantis* or the responsibility of the doer. In the Catechism we see the necessity of both: "From the moment that a sacrament is celebrated in accordance with the intention of the Church, the power of Christ and his Spirit acts in and through it, independently of the personal holiness of the minister. Nevertheless, the fruits of the sacraments also depend on the disposition of the one who receives them."[3] One cannot deny the lack of the fruits of the Sacraments in the life of the church. Again, our daunting statistics bear this out. How often do we hear this taught in our parishes? How often is the fruit of the Sacraments emphasized in our sacramental preparations? How long can we bear the erosion of this sacramental truth and not look toward radical change? If the faithful are to encounter Jesus Christ in the sacraments, and a culture of encounter is to be created in their reception, we must begin to emphasize the responsibility of the doer.

2. Weddell, *Forming Intentional Disciples*, 62.
3. *The Catechism of the Catholic Church*, 125, 1123, 1127, 1128.

Aquinas, in the *Summa Theologiae*, addresses the operation of the Sacraments. In studying his teaching on adult baptism, we can extrapolate principles which apply to all Sacraments. He identifies how several realities need to be present for the fruitful reception of a sacrament and also points out several issues that will block a sacrament from being fruitful. It is important to note one does not "take" a sacrament. I do not prepare myself to "take" Communion. Rather, I prepare myself to "receive" a sacrament. St. Thomas teaches us that a sacrament can be valid in form and matter, received, yet no fruit borne. Is this not a crisis and reality in our American churches?[4]

Repentance is the first action Aquinas points out must be operative in the life of the receiver. In baptism, he teaches this necessity before baptism. One of my disappointments in the Rite of Christian Initiation of Adults (RCIA) is to see the number of people who receive the Sacraments of Initiation and then disappear! I am familiar with many different programs of instruction of catechumens yet never see this specific emphasis brought to the catechumens. At best, repentance is mentioned, but many times as an academic exercise and not a life-changing event. The Greek word for repentance is *metanoia*, which is best translated to change your mind *and* to change your actions. This is different than the Greek word, *metamelomai*: to regret. Comparing these two words is worth noting. The distinctions so often laid down between these words seem hardly to be sustained by usage. However, *metanoia* is the fuller and nobler term, expressive of moral action and issues, indicated not only by its derivation, but by the greater frequency of its use and by the fact that it is often employed in the imperative (*metamelomai* is never used in the imperative).[5]

A stark example of these words becoming unclear in their English translations is the scripture in Matthew 27:3–4. Here we see the incident of Judas returning the thirty pieces of silver to the chief priests and the elders. "When Judas, his betrayer, saw that Jesus was condemned, he repented and brought back the thirty

4. Martin, "The Post-Christendom Sacramental Crisis," 64.
5. "*Metamelomai*," http://biblehub.com/greek/3338.htm.

THE ELEPHANT IN THE ROOM

pieces of silver to the chief priests and the elders. He said, 'I have sinned by betraying innocent blood.' But they said, 'What is that to us? See to it yourself.'" The Greek word here for "repent" is *metamelomai*. The translation should be "remorse" or "regret," not repent. Judas had remorse when Jesus was condemned, but there was no repentance. St. Thomas clearly teaches the kind of repentance needed in baptism is *metanoia*. Baptism does not include the sacrament of Penance. Baptism washes away all previous sin. You are free of sin. Confession follows the newly baptized once they receive the Sacraments of Initiation. Rather Aquinas is speaking of repentance that is pre-baptismal.

> In our present Catholic culture of sacramental preparation, the parish leaders most often assume that proper disposition is present in the person or persons prepared for the sacrament. Let's see how Aquinas disagrees: *A man is said to be insincere who makes a show of willing what he wills not. Now, whoever, approaches Baptism, by that very fact makes a show of having right faith in Christ, of veneration of this sacrament, and of wishing to conform to the Church, and to renounce sin. Consequently, to whatever sin a man wishes to cleave, if he approaches Baptism, he approaches insincerely, which is the same as to approach without devotion.*[6]

If, of course, the recipient receives baptism in an insincere manner and then later confesses in the sacrament of Penance, the graces of baptism are released to the baptized. St. Thomas comments on this as well: "In like manner, when a man is baptized, he receives the character, which is like a form: and he receives in consequence its proper effect, which is grace whereby all his sins are remitted. But this effect is sometimes hindered by insincerity. Wherefore, when this obstacle is removed by Penance, Baptism forthwith produces its effect."[7]

The focus on baptism relates to the other Sacraments as well. Remember the unique dynamic and posture in the Sacraments of

6. Martin, "The Post-Christendom Sacramental Crisis," 64.

7. Martin, "The Post-Christendom Sacramental Crisis," 64.

the doer is one of *receiving*. If repentance, which we often refer to as "ongoing conversion," is not present in the reception of all Sacraments, the fruit of that sacrament will not be realized. The one who receives must intend what the sacrament intends! This begins to give great pause when we see the number of baptized Catholics either becoming nonpracticing Catholics, leaving the faith altogether, or joining themselves to evangelical faith communities. We also note the damning statistics of the Confirmed, who through their teen years progressively detach from the church. There is no doubt a disconnect, even noted in the sacrament of Matrimony, between the giving of the Sacraments and the fruitful reception of them!

Someone has said many Catholics are catechized and "sacramentalized" but not evangelized! That would be one way to sum up the teaching of St. Thomas Aquinas and the truth of subjective disposition. The idea the sacrament will take care of itself, contrary to the disposition of he or she who receives, is totally false. We cannot expect a watered-down sacramental preparation to produce fruit; the call to repentance and faith in the Lord Jesus Christ must be the foundation of all formation. A Catholic priest from Cleveland told me of a member who continually came late to Sunday Mass and left after Eucharist. The priest decided to have a conversation with him and delve into his thinking. The parishioner stated, "Father, I got my sacrament!" Wow. I wonder if he did. I wonder if this is also the hope of so many catechists and those involved in religious education. I think the Pew Foundation has shown us that, indeed, many of our parishioners are not "getting their sacrament!"

There are also, I would suspect, bishops and priests who are not "getting their sacrament." Two years ago, I was at a meeting with the Coming Home Network, the EWTN apostolate that provides a bridge for Protestant clergy returning to the Catholic Church. They indeed were very helpful to me, personally, in my journey "home." At this conference, I had an extended conversation with a former Episcopal minister who became a Catholic priest. He had been amazed at how many times different Catholic priests approached him and wondered why he wanted to become a Catholic priest. They told him that there was no difference between what he has now and what he had before his Catholic ordination. It is interesting to note that Benedict XVI, when meeting with the bishops in their *"ad limina"* visits to the Vatican, described the New Evangelization as also a re-evangelization that must begin with the bishops themselves![8] If the church culture is to change dramatically into a culture of encounter, all of us from bishops, to the priests, to the deacons, to religious, to laity, must settle for no less than an initial or a renewing encounter with the person and work of our Lord Jesus Christ!

YOUR CHALLENGE

To those who prepare others for receiving Sacraments, catechize the truth about the responsibility of not only proper form and matter but also the fruitfulness of the sacrament in the life of the recipient based upon one's sincerity.

8. Kerr, "Benedict XVI Tells New York Bishops."

Chapter 6

Eucharistic Amazement

> I would like to rekindle this Eucharistic "amazement" by
> the present Encyclical Letter, in continuity with the Jubilee
> heritage which I have left to the Church in the Apostolic Letter
> Novo Millennio Ineunte and its Marian crowning, Rosarium
> Virginis Mariae. To contemplate the face of Christ, and to
> contemplate it with Mary, is the "programme" which I have
> set before the Church at the dawn of the third millennium,
> summoning her to put out into the deep on the sea of history
> with the enthusiasm of the new evangelization.[1]

WITH THIS GOAL, St. Pope John Paul II called the church to renew
her ardor for the Eucharist, the source and summit of our faith. On
Thursday, June 10, 2004, when celebrating Corpus Christi with the
Diocese of Rome, St. Pope John Paul II announced that in October
2004, coinciding with the International Eucharistic Congress of
Guadalajara, Mexico, a special Year of the Eucharist would begin,
which would end in October 2005 with the ordinary assembly
of the Synod of Bishops, whose theme would be "The Eucharist:
Source and Summit of the Life and Mission of the Church."

---

1. John Paul, *Encyclical Letter, Ecclesia de Eucharistia*, para. 6.

The Holy Father explained that this is in line with the pastoral project he presented in his apostolic letter for the new millennium, in which he invited the faithful to "start afresh from Christ": "Contemplating more assiduously the countenance of the Incarnate Word, really present in the Sacrament, they will be able to exercise themselves in the art of prayer, and commit themselves in that high degree of the Christian life which is the indispensable condition to develop in an effective manner the new evangelization."[2] The phrase "starting afresh from Christ" is prophetic for God's people in the Catholic Church. The reception of the Eucharist, in the faith generated in John 6 of the Gospels, will do that very thing! As mentioned in chapter 2, I had a significant encounter with the Eucharistic Jesus while serving as an altar boy. When I returned to the Lord in that poignant moment in college, I returned to him but not to the Great Church. Unfortunately, the Sacraments did not have a place in my spiritual life for the next thirty years! This created a void in my spiritual life that could not be filled. During this time of Evangelical Christianity, I implemented weekly communion in my Christian communities, whereas most all the other communities at best had communion quarterly or yearly. There was something in my spiritual DNA that longed for the Real Presence and the Source and Summit of the faith. One Sunday, after our meeting, a college student came to me with an observation. Away at college, he only came to our services during breaks. He noted in our conversation: "Pastor Doane, this community is looking more like the Catholic Church every time I come to services." It was during this period I began to read the Apostolic Fathers. These are the saints of the second century. Men like Ignatius, Polycarp, and Irenaeus were writing about the faith given to them by the Apostles.[3] These were men who were disciples of the Apostles. I was amazed to read them as they spoke of bishops and the Real Presence of Jesus in the Eucharist. Eucharistic amazement was beginning to stir my soul.

Ten years ago, on Easter Sunday, my wife and I returned to the church and the Sacraments. I continue to be amazed and surprised

2. John Paul, *Encyclical Letter, Ecclesia de Eucharistia*, para. 6.

3. Sparks, *The Apostolic Fathers*, x.

at the experience of eating his flesh and drinking his blood. In the early church, one of the reasons Rome persecuted the church was because they said the Christians practiced cannibalism.[4] There always has been a stigma attached to this sacrament. St. Paul told us that the cross would be foolishness to the Gentiles. In the Eucharist, we find the clear connection to the Cross of Christ, for the Apostle told us that when we eat his Flesh and drink his Blood, we unite most directly to the Passion.

> For I received from the Lord what I also handed on to you, that the Lord Jesus on the night when he was betrayed took a loaf of bread, and when he had given thanks, he broke it and said, "This is my body that is for you. Do this in remembrance of me." In the same way, he took the cup also, after supper, saying, "This cup is the new covenant in my blood. Do this, as often as you drink it, in remembrance of me." *For as often as you eat this bread and drink the cup, you proclaim the Lord's death until he comes.* (1 Cor 11:23–26, emphasis added)

Many stopped following Jesus in John 6 because of his call to the Eucharist. "Very truly, I tell you, unless you eat the flesh of the Son of Man and drink his blood, you have no life in you" (John 6:53).

An interesting note on this: another great surprise in returning to the Eucharist was the connection between the Eucharist and the sacrament of Penance. If one would have told me ten years ago that an important part of my spiritual life would be receiving the sacrament of Penance on a regular basis, I would have thought they were crazy! But I have discovered these two sacraments have a direct connection, and to have the fullness of the Eucharist, we must be people who encounter the risen Lord in the sacrament of Penance. In the Gospel of John, the writer records the Apostles with Jesus in the upper room both at the institution of the Eucharist before his death and then at the institution of the

---

4. "Why Early Christians Were Despised," https://www.christianity.com/church/church-history/timeline/1-300/why-early-christians-were-despised-11629610.html.

sacrament of Penance in that same upper room immediately after his resurrection.

Finally, the Lord, from the beginning, has always put up a guard or fence to protect his Holy Presence. In the garden, he put an angel to guard the Tree of Life after Adam and Eve disobeyed the Lord and were put out of the garden. With Moses, the Lord told him to take off his shoes because he was on holy ground. The Lord said the same thing when appearing to Joshua before the crossing into the Promised Land. Also, Moses, when he asked God to see his Presence in the mountain, the Lord stated he could not let Moses see his face, for he would die. However, God passed by him and let Moses see his backside. In the wilderness, the people constructed a mobile tabernacle, and only the high priest could enter the Holy of Holies once a year. The whole tabernacle was surrounded by a fence seven feet high and covered with badger skins, so no one outside could see into this sacred space. In fact, the Holy of Holies (also called the Holy Place, Exod 28:35) was the most sacred area of the tabernacle or the temple. The high priest could enter this room only once a year on the Day of Atonement. When he entered, he had to wear the clothes that God specified in Exodus 28. If he did not, he would die. We do know that bells, blue and purple pomegranates, and scarlet material were attached to the bottom of the high priest's garment. If God's people could hear the bells, they knew the high priest's offering was acceptable to God. If the bells stopped ringing, then the high priest had died because God's Presence was not honored correctly. The temple was built with the same attention to detail to protect the Holy Presence. Now all these types have been fulfilled in Jesus in the Eucharist. In 1 Corinthians 11:17–33, we read St. Paul's teaching on the Eucharist. He is addressing the Corinthians who were not receiving the Eucharist in a *worthy* manner. He stated in this context that, first, a person must examine himself or herself before receiving the sacrament. Here is a clear implication for the necessity of the sacrament of Penance. He goes on to teach that the Eucharist can be received either in a worthy or an unworthy manner. Because many in the Corinthian church were receiving in an unworthy manner, some were weak, some were ill, and some had died (1 Cor 11:30)! That is amazing! The Lord's Presence is not fictional. The Lord has been putting a guard around his Presence from time immemorial. The Holy Spirit continues to defend the Holy of Holies, which has found its ultimate fulfillment in the Source and Summit of our faith—the Holy Eucharist! Creating a culture of encounter here is at its highest level!

YOUR CHALLENGE

To the clergy—your responsibility is to instruct the people of God about the sacredness of God's Presence in the Eucharist. Do not neglect St. Paul's instructions in 1 Corinthians 11 concerning receiving the Eucharist in a worthy manner!

Chapter 7

Going Forward Means Going Backward

C. S. Lewis made a keen observation in his classic writing, *Mere Christianity*.

> First, as to putting the clock back. Would you think I was joking if I said that you can put a clock back and that if the clock is wrong, it is often a very sensible thing to do? But I would rather get away from that whole idea of clocks. We all want progress. But progress means getting nearer to the place where you want to be. And if you have taken a wrong turning, then to go forward does not get you any nearer. If you are on the wrong road, progress means doing an about turn and walking back to the right road; and in that case the man who turns back soonest is the most progressive man. We have all seen this when doing arithmetic. When I have started a sum the wrong way, the sooner I admit this and go back and start over again, the faster I shall get on. There is nothing progressive about being pigheaded and refusing to admit a mistake. And I think if you look at the present state of the world, it is pretty plain that humanity has been making some big mistakes. We are on the wrong road. And if that is so, we must go back. Going back is the quickest way on.[1]

1. Lewis, *Mere Christianity*, book 1:5, para. 2.

When I first read this quote, several years ago, it gripped me. It made me reflect upon my journey, thus far, and different places I may have taken a wrong road or path. It has been healthy for me to keep this perspective as I reflect on my life. I believe, to encounter Jesus and create a culture of encounter, we must go backward, first to the sacred Scriptures and specifically to the Acts of the Apostles. As mentioned in my introduction, the Acts of the Apostles should be looked at as the model for Catholic spirituality and culture building. It is a practical handbook that gives us context to implement new initiatives from John Paul the Great's call for a new evangelization: *new in ardor, new in methods,* and *new in expression.* Just as there is a movement within the confines of Catholic theology to "return to the Fathers of the Church" so too, if we are to create a culture of encounter, we must return to Acts to see what this culture looks like in its earliest and foundational form.[2]

In the "great commission" of Matthew 28:19–20 Jesus commanded the disciples to "Go." But in Acts, he tells them not to depart but to "Wait." What were they to wait for? An encounter with the Holy Spirit! In Acts 1:8, he goes on to explain they will receive power when the Holy Spirit comes upon them, and they will *then* become his witnesses. The Acts of the Apostles, therefore, serves as a prototype for the encounter with the risen Lord. Acts 1:8 becomes the lens through which we draw upon this writing and discover or uncover the spirituality required to create a culture of encounter! I believe the interpretative key for the entire Acts of the Apostles narrative is the Acts 1:8 passage: "But you will receive power when the Holy Spirit has come upon you; and you will be my witnesses in Jerusalem, in all Judea and Samaria, and to the ends of the earth." The Holy Spirit and his ongoing "coming upon" the church has always been and continues to be a non-negotiable for all activity and the advance of God's kingdom. There are some who have referred to the Holy Spirit as the neglected person within the Trinity. In the Apostles' Creed, written around AD 180, the Holy Spirit gets one short line: "I believe in the Holy Spirit." Later, in the fourth century, his status seems to increase with the Nicene/Constantinople Creed:

2. "Changing Perspectives in Catholic Theology."

"I believe in the Holy Spirit, the Lord and Giver of life, who proceeds from the Father and the Son, together with the Father and Son is adored and glorified. He has spoken through the prophets."[3]

In the Acts of the Apostles (many like the name Acts of the Holy Spirit, instead) one reads the Holy Spirit as anything but neglected or forgotten. He is the center of activity constantly speaking to, working with, and empowering the new believers. He is encountering and meeting the people of God. Throughout the twenty-eight chapters in the writing, the Holy Spirit is specifically mentioned forty times! Therefore, first, there needs to be a restoration of emphasis, conversation, prayer to, and encounter with the Holy Spirit in the church. This encounter will show itself forth in changed lives and human tinder ignited by the flames of God. What is the evidence of being baptized and filled continually with the Spirit? How do I know he has touched me? Let us look to St. John Paul the Great for some insights as to the evidence of the Spirit's presence:

> The first confirmation of this promise of Jesus will be had on the day of Pentecost and the subsequent days, as the Acts of the Apostles attests. The promise is not limited to the apostles and their immediate companions in evangelization. It extends to the future generations of disciples and confessors of Christ. The Gospel is destined for all nations and for all the successive generations which will arise in the context of diverse cultures and of the manifold progress of human civilization. Viewing the whole range of history Jesus said: "The Spirit of truth who proceeds from the Father will bear witness to me" (John 15:26). "He will bear witness," that is to say, he will show the true meaning of the Gospel within the Church, so that she may proclaim it authentically to the whole world. Always and everywhere, even in the ceaselessly changing events of the life of humanity, the "Spirit of truth" will guide the Church "into all the truth" (John 16:13).[4]

So, the first evidence seen through the pope's insight is the lifting up and bearing witness to Jesus. Both in and outside of the

3. Pelikan and Hotchkiss, *Creeds & Confessions*, 160–61.

4. John Paul, "The Spirit of Truth."

church, the name of Jesus needs to be lifted! When filled with God's Spirit, the name will ring out in individual conversations, in families, in small fellowship groups, in the pulpits of parishes, from bishops' chairs, and finally in the streets and marketplaces of nations.

St. John Paul goes on to say:

> The relationship between the revelation communicated by the Holy Spirit and that of Jesus is very close. It is not a question of a different disparate revelation. This can be deduced from the actual words of Christ's promise: "The Counselor, the Holy Spirit, whom the Father will send in my name will teach you all things and bring to your remembrance all that I have said to you" (John 14:26). The "bringing to remembrance" is the function of memory. By recalling, one returns to what has been, to what has been said and done, thus renewing the awareness of things past, and as it were, making them live again. In regard to the Holy Spirit, the Spirit of a truth endowed with divine power, his mission is not limited to recalling the past as such. "By recalling" the words, deeds and the entire salvific mystery of Christ, the Spirit of truth makes him continually present in the Church. The Spirit ensures that He takes on an ever new "reality" in the community of salvation. Thanks to the action of the Holy Spirit, the Church not only recalls the truth, but remains and lives in the truth received from her Lord. The words of Christ are fulfilled also in this way: "He (the Holy Spirit) will bear witness to me" (John 15:26). This witness of the Spirit of truth is thus identified with the presence of the ever living Christ, with the active power of the Gospel, with the redemption increasingly put into effect and with a continual exposition of truth and virtue. In this way the Holy Spirit "guides" the Church "into all the truth." The *Church goes out to meet the glorious Christ.*[5]

The second evidence of the Holy Spirit's activity is that the faithful recover the Spirit's work and do not relegate it to past ages. When I read the Scripture, I can honestly place myself there, in the here and now. Like St. Ignatius Loyola taught us, the characters

5. John Paul, "The Spirit of Truth."

of the Scripture are alive and can be emulated by us today. As the pope said, we make the things said and done in former days live again! This will be a great adventure!

A third evidence is a hope and a victorious eschatology:

> Again, Jesus said: "The Spirit of truth . . . will declare to you the things that are to come" (John 16:13). What is the meaning of this prophetic and eschatological projection? In it, Jesus placed under the ray of the Holy Spirit the entire future of the Church, the entire historical journey it is called upon to carry out down the centuries. It means going to meet the glorious Christ, toward whom it reaches out as expressed in the invocation inspired by the Spirit: "Come, Lord Jesus!" (Revelation 22:17, 20). The Holy Spirit leads the Church toward a constant progress in understanding of revealed truth. He watches over the teaching of that truth, over its preservation and over its application to changing historical situations. He stirs up and guides the development of all that serves the knowledge and spread of that truth, particularly in scriptural exegesis and theological research. These can never be separated from the guidance of the Spirit of truth nor from the Magisterium of the Church, in which the Spirit is always at work.[6]

Just as when St. Peter walked on the water, we tend to look at the storm and the waves and take our eyes off Jesus. The result is a sinking hope and a culture of death and futility. The evidence of the Holy Spirit in our lives is a great hope and expectation for now and the future. I have read the back of the "book" and discovered something: Jesus wins!

Finally, as the pope taught concerning the Spirit's work, there will be a great faith rising in our hearts, words, and lives:

> Everything happens in faith and through faith under the action of the Holy Spirit, as was stated in the encyclical Dominum et Vivificantem: "For the mystery of Christ taken as a whole demands faith, since it is faith that adequately introduces man into the reality of the revealed mystery. The 'guiding into all the truth' is therefore achieved in faith

6. John Paul, "The Spirit of Truth."

and through faith: and this is the work of the Spirit of truth and the result of his action in man. Here the Holy Spirit is to be man's supreme guide and the light of the human spirit. This holds true for the apostles, the eyewitnesses, who must now bring to all people the proclamation of what Christ did and taught, and especially the proclamation of his cross and resurrection. Taking a longer view, this also holds true for all the generations of disciples and confessors of the Master, since they will have to accept with faith and confess with candor the mystery of God at work in human history, the revealed mystery which explains the definitive meaning of that history."[7]

So, we accept with faith and confess with candor the mystery of God at work, today, in our human history. When a man or woman, clergy, religious, and laity, parish, and diocese are filled with God's Spirit, we shall see these four things. First, we will bear witness to the name of Jesus. Second, a spirituality will emerge that demonstrates the power, enthusiasm, boldness, and character of the apostolic church. Third, we shall see an abandonment to the Lord concerning our personal and corporate futures, knowing the Lord governs the nations and is in control. Convenience and comfort will be replaced by risk and suffering. Last, the fourth evidence will be a rising of personal and corporate faith so as to become confessors of the Master!

Come, Holy Spirit!

YOUR CHALLENGE

Seek the infilling of the Holy Spirit! Bow before him and invoke his presence. Ask Jesus to give you more of the Holy Spirit in your life!

In January of 1980, John Paul II told a group from the Charismatic Renewal:

> From the time I was little, I learned to pray to the Holy Spirit. When I was 11, I was feeling sad because I was having a lot of trouble with math. My dad showed me in a little book the hymn "Veni Creator Spiritus," and he told me,

7. John Paul, "The Spirit of Truth."

"Pray this and you'll see that He'll help you to understand."
I've been praying this hymn every day for more than 40
years, and I've seen how much the Divine Spirit helps us.

Come, Holy Spirit, Creator blest,
and in our souls take up Thy rest;
come with Thy grace and heavenly aid
to fill the hearts which Thou hast made.
O comforter, to Thee we cry,
O heavenly gift of God Most High,
O fount of life and fire of love,
and sweet anointing from above.
Thou in Thy sevenfold gifts are known;
Thou, finger of God's hand we own;
Thou, promise of the Father, Thou
Who dost the tongue with power imbue.
Kindle our sense from above,
and make our hearts o'erflow with love;
with patience firm and virtue high
the weakness of our flesh supply.
Far from us drive the foe we dread,
and grant us Thy peace instead;
so shall we not, with Thee for guide,
turn from the path of life aside.
Oh, may Thy grace on us bestow
the Father and the Son to know;
and Thee, through endless times confessed,
of both the eternal Spirit blest.
Now to the Father and the Son,
Who rose from death, be glory given,
with Thou, O Holy Comforter,
henceforth by all in earth and heaven. Amen.[8]

8. "This is a Prayer John Paul II Prayed Every Day."

Chapter 8

Discovering the Secret

JESUS TAUGHT US CLEARLY, in the Sermon on the Mount, to go and find the secret place of prayer. There, our heavenly Father, who sees in secret, will reward us (Matt 6:5–6). Prayer is our daily encounter with Jesus Christ and tills the ground for ongoing encounters throughout the day. Of course, Jesus is our ultimate example of this: "In the morning, while it was still very dark, He got up and went out to a deserted place, and there He prayed" (Mark 1:35). Private prayer and public prayer (including the Mass) are two sides of one coin. Although some people may suggest one being more valuable than another, sacred Scripture does not offer that dichotomy. Rather, both play a critical part in the culture of encounter.

If we continue to allow the Acts of the Apostles to be our teacher and form the basis of our spirituality, we discover both private and public prayer as irreplaceable in the life of the church. Acts 2:42 tells us that corporate, public prayers were a part of the new church's lifestyle and culture. Pew research has uncovered an interesting statistic that deserves reflection. While only 25 percent of American Catholics attend Mass on a weekly basis, and 60 percent fall into the range of a few times a year/seldom and never, 59 percent of Catholics pray daily and 20 percent pray weekly![1] There is a spiritual tinder box that will ignite if a new culture presents itself on the American Catholic terrain. How does a praying Catholic Church appear? Again, the Acts becomes our tutor into this vital part of our Catholic spirituality. Acts 1:14 immediately tells us after the ascension of Jesus to heaven, the disciples returned to Mount Olivet and the upper room for a distinct purpose: with one accord, to devote themselves to prayer. They were in the company of Mary, the mother of Jesus, and his kin. It was during this time that Mathias was chosen to replace Judas. It was here, ten days after the ascension, that the Holy Spirit fell on the 120, and the church was born! Public, communal prayer formed the milieu in which God moved in a mighty way. This kind of prayer happens time and time again in this seminal book, and it is no coincidence the Holy Spirit's activity is in direct response to this. An old preacher in my young days as a minister would often say, "God doesn't do the work all on his own and neither do we; rather, we do it together!"

We continue to see this picture of corporate prayer and intercession in the life of the apostolic church. In Acts 4, Peter and John are brought before the Jewish Council because of the healing of the lame beggar in front of the temple. After being threatened and released, the two of them returned to their brethren to report the incident. Immediately they all lifted their voices in prayer, together.

Rather than asking for relief, they petitioned God for more boldness and for him to give them power for healing, signs, and wonders. "When they had prayed, the place in which they were gathered together was shaken; and they were all filled with the Holy Spirit and spoke the word of God with boldness" (Acts 4:31).

We see this pattern throughout these early days:

- The apostolic job description of prayer and ministry of the word (Acts 6:4). The choice of the first deacons (Acts 6:6).

- Peter and James thrown in prison with James killed by the sword and Peter rescued by an angel. Earnest prayer was

1. O'Loughlin, "Pew survey," and www.pewforum.org/religious-landscape -study/frequency-of-prayer/.

made for him by the church. His release from prison took place while the believers prayed at Mary's house. "While Peter was kept in prison, the church prayed fervently to God for him" (Acts 12:5, 12).

- St. Paul and St. Barnabas commissioned for their first missionary journey (Acts 13:2). The conversion of Lydia at a place of prayer at the riverside (Acts 16:13).

- The casting out of divination from the slave girl took place as they were heading to the place of prayer (Acts 16:16).

- Paul and Silas caused an earthquake through their prayers that led to the conversion of the Philippian jailor (Acts 16:25).

- A powerful scene with St. Paul ended in corporate, public prayer: "When he had finished speaking, he knelt down with them all and prayed. There was much weeping among them all; they embraced Paul and kissed him, grieving especially because of what he had said, that they would not see him again. Then they brought him to the ship" (Acts 20:36–38). Paul left the Ephesians, while all knew they would not see one another again.

This pattern of easily and frequently experiencing corporate and public prayer that is targeted in each situation is lacking in many lives of Catholics and parishes. Beyond attending daily Mass, citing the Angelus, and opening and closing public meetings with written prayers, there seems to be a lack of urgency and consistency in our prayers.

Intercession is one of our lost treasures. Several years ago, an American Chinese Christian related a story to me I have never forgotten. He was visiting underground Chinese house churches in the rural areas where Catholic and Evangelical Christianity are both proliferating. He went to bed one evening and woke up at 5:00 a.m. to a "buzzing sound." He went down the stairs of this family dwelling to find the lower level covered with believers lying prostrate on the floor praying and interceding before the Lord. Many reports coming to us from China tell us the faith is spreading like

wildfire, and many signs and wonders are taking place. This "buzzing" must again resound in our churches.

It is well to note that the corporate or public prayer in Acts is
not soley in meetings for the "breaking of bread," with the possibility of Acts 13:2 as an exception. Rather, we see believers gravitating
to public prayer in houses, on beaches, in jails, on roadways, and
at the river's edge. To bring this culture back to the church, clergy,
religious, and laity will need to become bold in calling the faithful
to pray always and in all places. This will be prayer highlighted
by intercession and not just recitation. Joining prayer groups will
become normative and not the rarity it is now. Praying publicly
can be as small as what Jesus mentioned in Matthew 18:20: "For
where two or three are gathered together in my name, there am I
in the midst of them."

Let me end these thoughts with a story. When my wife and
I returned to the Catholic Church ten years ago, the first thing we
did was meet with two Catholic leaders on separate occasions.
We told our stories and journey and how the Lord was leading
us back to the church. In both instances, at the end of the time
together, neither leader led us in prayer in their offices. My wife
and I went away from those instances with a pause, wondering
why no prayers were offered at the end of a very poignant time
for us in our journey. We have come to realize, with exceptions of
course, that prayer, outside the liturgy, is often not present in many
Catholic settings. This will need to change!

Not only do we discover a culture of public prayer and encounter in the Acts of the Apostles, but the Spirit records much
private prayer as well. Again, the two go hand in hand. One without the other limits what God can do in both our personal lives
and in the life of our parishes. Just as Jesus modeled private prayer
for us in the Gospels, so the disciples formed by him and their
followers demonstrated a prayer life tied to their personal and ongoing encounter with Jesus Christ.

St. James the Just, the Bishop of Rome and principal spokes-
man at the Jerusalem Council in Acts 15, and kinsman of our Lord
received the nickname Old Camel Knees because of his devotion

to private prayer. His knees became so calloused because of his prayer life they looked like the knees of a camel![2] It was this personal piety and spirituality within the apostolic church that we too should model if Catholic culture is to be renewed.

A survey of private prayer in Acts reveals private prayer at significant junctures in the life and growth of the church. First, we see the great St. Paul, immediately after his conversion, while still blind, engrossed in prayer:

> Now there was a disciple in Damascus named Ananias. The Lord said to him in a vision, "Ananias." He answered, "Here I am, Lord." The Lord said to him, "Get up and go to the street called Straight, and at the house of Judas look for a man of Tarsus named Saul. At this moment he is praying, and he has seen in a vision a man named Ananias come in and lay his hands on him so that he might regain his sight. But Ananias answered, "Lord, I have heard from many about this man, how much evil he has done to your saints in Jerusalem; and here he has authority from the chief priests to bind all who invoke your name." But the Lord said to him, "Go, for he is an instrument whom I have chosen to bring my name before Gentiles and kings and before the people of Israel; I myself will show him how much he must suffer for the sake of my name." (Acts 9: 10–16)

So here, the man apprehended by God prayed in preparation for his immense call and mission. So too will our individual call and mission unfold and take place within this kind of personal piety.

St. Peter showed the power of a personal prayer life when he entered Joppa, led by the Holy Spirit, for the raising of Dorcas and then the revelation that Gentiles were included in the new church.

> Since Lydda was near Joppa, the disciples, who heard that Peter was there, sent two men to him with the request, "Please come to us without delay." So Peter got up and went with them; and when he arrived, they took

2. "All the Men of the Bible—James," https://www.biblegateway.com/resources/all-men-bible/James.

him to the room upstairs. All the widows stood beside him, weeping and showing tunics and other clothing that Dorcas had made while she was with them. Peter put all of them outside, and then he knelt down and prayed. He turned to the body and said, "Tabitha, get up." Then she opened her eyes, and seeing Peter, she sat up. He gave her his hand and helped her up. Then calling the saints and widows, he showed her to be alive. This became known throughout Joppa, and many believed in the Lord. Meanwhile he stayed in Joppa for some time with a certain Simon, a tanner." (Acts 9:38–43)

We often wonder where this power is today. Because there was such a culture of private prayer, the healings, signs, and wonders were a part of the apostolic ministry.

From the healing of Dorcas, St. Peter moved on to stay at the house of Simon, the tanner. At the same time, there was a Roman centurion in Caesarea who had the reputation of liberally giving alms and praying constantly.

In Caesarea, there was a man named Cornelius, a centurion of the Italian Cohort, as it was called. He was a devout man who feared God with all his household; he gave alms generously to the people and prayed constantly to God. One afternoon at about three o'clock he had a vision in which he clearly saw an angel of God coming in and saying to him, "Cornelius." He stared at him in terror and said, "What is it, Lord?" He answered, "Your prayers and your alms have ascended as a memorial before God. Now send men to Joppa for a certain Simon who is called Peter; he is lodging with Simon, a tanner, whose house is by the seaside." When the angel who spoke to him had left, he called two of his slaves and a devout soldier from the ranks of those who served him, and after telling them everything, he sent them to Joppa." (Acts 10:1–8)

It amazes me that a nonbelieving Gentile prayed regularly, and those prayers, along with his alms, created a memorial before God! Simultaneously, Peter focused on his private prayer and entered the grand scheme of God's purpose. While in private prayer,

Peter fell into a trance. He received from God a vision he did not understand until he later arrived at the house of Cornelius.

> About noon the next day, as they were on their journey and approaching the city, Peter went up on the roof to pray. He became hungry and wanted something to eat; and while it was being prepared, he fell into a trance. He saw the heavens opened and something like a large sheet coming down, being lowered to the ground by its four corners. In it were all kinds of four-footed creatures and reptiles and birds of the air. Then he heard a voice saying, "Get up, Peter; kill and eat." But Peter said, "By no means, Lord; for I have never eaten anything that is profane or unclean." The voice said to him again, a second time, "What God has made clean, you must not call profane." This happened three times, and the thing was suddenly taken up to heaven. (Acts 10:9–16, 11.4–5)

The amazing orchestration of the Holy Spirit that brought the Gentiles into the kingdom of God through the preaching of the *kerygma* by St. Peter was dependent on the *private prayers* of both Cornelius and the Apostle! Are we, as twenty-first-century Catholics, able to project and see the potential and awesome power which would take place if a new generation of Catholic Christians developed "camel knees"?

It is worth noting, St. Paul, too, was praying at the temple, after receiving his sight. He fell into a trance and saw the Lord, who directed him to leave Jerusalem (Acts 22:17). So here also, private prayer led to divine guidance that preserved St. Paul and led him to the focus of his ministry—the Gentiles!

It is evident to me and hopefully to you, the reader, the renewal of American and possibly all Western Catholicism will depend on a movement of private and public prayer. May God help us to make no substitute for this culture and lifestyle, and may the Holy Spirit inspire all of us to pray! John Paul the Great expresses well the need for these two kinds of prayer to be at the heart of Catholic culture:

If in the planning that awaits us we commit ourselves more confidently to a pastoral activity that gives personal and communal prayer its proper place we shall be observing an essential principle of the Christian view of life: the primacy of grace . . . But it is fatal to forget that "without Christ we can do nothing" (cf. John. 15:5). It is prayer which roots us in this truth. It constantly reminds us of the primacy of Christ and, in union, with him, the primacy of the interior life and of holiness. When this principle is not respected, is it any wonder that pastoral plans come to nothing and leave us with a disheartening sense of frustration?[3]

YOUR CHALLENGE

Consistent personal prayer begins with a Rule or "fixed prayers" or "liturgical prayers" that are said daily. The Our Father is a good example of a fixed prayer. Personal prayer is developed on the foundation of the corporate life of the church—it is not a substitute for regular participation in the Mass and sacraments. However, corporate prayer at Mass cannot take the place of personal prayer. A Rule of prayer is the "framework" which guides one regularly as he or she prays personally.[4]

3. John Paul, *Apostolic Letter Novo millennio*, 38.

4. Dunaway, *Building a Habit of Prayer*, 1.

Chapter 9

Encountering Jesus in the Unseen War

> Then I saw heaven opened, and there was a white horse! Its rider is called Faithful and True, and in righteousness he judges and makes war. His eyes are like a flame of fire, and on his head are many diadems; and he has a name inscribed that no one knows but himself. He is clothed in a robe dipped in blood, and his name is called The Word of God. And the armies of heaven, wearing fine linen, white and pure, were following him on white horses. From his mouth comes a sharp sword with which to strike down the nations, and he will rule them with a rod of iron; he will tread the wine press of the fury of the wrath of God the Almighty. On his robe and on his thigh, he has a name inscribed, "King of kings and Lord of lords."
>
> REV 19:11–16

CATHOLICS, EVEN THE MOST devout, often find themselves "flat-footed" and unengaged in the unseen war happening around them. Having returned to the church ten years ago, I have yet to hear a homily on spiritual warfare, dealing with the devil, resisting demons, or wearing my spiritual armor. Starting in the book of

Genesis with the serpent, and ending with Revelation 20:10, where Satan is cast into the lake of fire forever, the Scripture unveils for us an unseen war in which every person must and will participate. In this chapter, I wish to focus on dealing with our enemy, Satan.

In our encounter with Jesus Christ, we are brought into the spiritual realm where we are called to deal with our enemies. We have two other enemies we must confront, namely the world and the flesh (Jas 4:1–10). These three enemies are the totality of our warfare and cause the church on earth to be called the church militant. For our Catholicism to renew, each of us will have to "volunteer" to fight in God's army by identifying the enemy of our souls, becoming knowledgeable of his schemes, discovering our spiritual weapons and how to use them, and finally entering the battle.[1]

Volunteering to fight in God's army against the archenemy of Jesus Christ is a call to all of us, men and women both, to engage in warfare. We have no choice. There are no pacifists in this war; no one can escape the sound of war. The Scripture gives us clear instruction.

> Discipline yourselves, keep alert. Like a roaring lion your adversary the devil prowls around, looking for someone to devour. Resist him, steadfast in your faith, for you know that your brothers and sisters in all the world are undergoing the same kinds of suffering. And after you have suffered for a little while, the God of all grace, who has called you to his eternal glory in Christ, will himself restore, support, strengthen, and establish you." (1 Pet 5:8–10)

Here we see several elements that are the ingredients in this unseen warfare. First, we need to be vigilant, on the alert, and sober. A discipline of regular prayer and Scripture reading in personal piety, as well as faithful attendance at Sunday Eucharist and consistent participation in the sacrament of Penance, and our corporate devotion, allows us to be spiritually alert and not asleep.

One of the enemy's critical attacks is to make us feel guilty. In Revelation 12 we are told that he is the "accuser of the brethren,

---

1. Thigpen, *Manual for Spiritual Warfare*,

accusing them before God, day and night." The sacrament of Penance delivers a death blow to Satan's accusations.

Volunteering to engage the enemy of our souls means recognizing that the devil is real and wants to *devour* me, my faith, my family, and my future. My response is summed up in one word—*resist*. Catholics often accept the lie of secularism that explains that the devil was a way to describe evil to culturally illiterate populations. C. S. Lewis, in his classic *The Screwtape Letters*, points out one of the enemy's key strategies: "I wonder you should ask me whether it is essential to keep the patient in ignorance of your own existence. That question, at least for the present phase of the struggle, has been answered for us by the High Command. Our policy, for the moment, is to conceal ourselves. Of course, this has not always been so."[2]

Once we acknowledge the truth of the devil's existence and his desire to "devour" us, we next must uncover his schemes and how he plans to neutralize us. Jesus clearly stated the devil's strategies. First, speaking to the Pharisees he described the nature of Satan. "You are from your father the devil, and you choose to do your father's desires. He was a murderer from the beginning and does not stand in the truth, because there is no truth in him. When he lies, he speaks according to his own nature, for he is a liar and the father of lies" (John 8:44). Earlier, in John 10:10, Jesus revealed to us the plans of the evil one: "The thief comes only *to steal, kill and destroy*. I came that they may have life and have it abundantly" (emphasis added). We see, therefore, his nature, and then we see his plans. This is who each of us must *confront*. He is a murderer, there is no truth in him or about him, and his nature is to lie. In fact, he is the source of lies! He comes, and when he comes, it is to steal, kill, and destroy (for indeed as 1 Peter states, he actively looks for those he can devour). To either deny or neglect this reality in our existence is to be defeated! When speaking of the schemes of the devil, sacred Scripture uses English words like *designs, craftiness,* and *wiles*. We deal with an intelligent fallen angel who leads a vast army whose intention is first to destroy you and me and to keep us

2. Lewis, *The Screwtape Letters*, 32.

from a living faith in Jesus Christ. If he fails in the first part of this strategy, the next step is to make us ineffective in serving the Lord.

To resist his temptations, we will need to take seriously the call of Ephesians 6 to put on the full armor of God. The primary field of battle where he comes to us is our mind. The mind is where we need to be on alert, every day and in every circumstance. When he comes and entices us in our minds, we must ask ourselves how he does this and what his temptations are. Again, our Lord's experience in the Scripture gives us insight. When Jesus went into the wilderness, we learned exactly what the enemy's schemes are and the areas in which he attacks. He tempted our Lord in three specific areas: the desires of the *flesh, the world, and the devil, himself.* Abusing pleasures, lusting for power, and loving wealth and false worship were offered. These realms are the places of Satan's schemes. We must learn from the Lord's example if we are to be indeed successful and defeat the evil one and his plots against us.

Jesus resisted the devil by applying the Scripture to each temptation. This is the only language the devil cannot undo. Scripture is the language that strips him of power in his enticements. If we approach him with human thoughts only, he will undo us. If we take an approach toward evil that says, "If you leave me alone, I will leave you alone," Satan will crush us. So, how do we engage the battle? We discover our spiritual armor and put it on!

When we become Christians, we are automatically involved in a vast spiritual war both in heaven and on Earth. Furthermore, our most powerful and dangerous enemies are a kingdom of evil angels whose headquarters are in the unseen realm of creation. In his wisdom and mercy, God has provided us with all the weapons that we need to accomplish victory. Because our warfare is in the spiritual realm, our weapons are also spiritual. In 2 Corinthians 10:4, Paul says that "the weapons of our warfare are not carnal [but by implication, spiritual] but mighty in God for pulling down strongholds." The strongholds that we attack are also spiritual. Over the centuries, Satan has built these strongholds in the hearts and minds of humanity. They are strongholds of fear, covetousness, hatred, idolatry, racism, religious superstition, atheism, and pride. These strongholds frustrate all the attempts of present-day politicians to negotiate a lasting peace. Real peace will only come when the kingdom of Christ comes. The objective of our warfare as Catholic Christians and the purpose for which we use our spiritual weapons is to destroy strongholds. Our call, as a community, is to tear down the spiritual strongholds in the hearts of men and women and to prepare the way for Christ to set up his kingdom—first in their hearts and finally in the whole earth.[3]

In Ephesians 6:13–18, St. Paul lists seven spiritual weapons or items of spiritual equipment that we need. When we "put on" the armor of Ephesians, we can then *resist* the devil, as we are told in James 4:7, and make headway in spiritual warfare. Paul takes his examples from the equipment of a Roman legionary in his day.[4]

First, he tells us to *put on* "*the girdle of truth*" (Eph 6:14, emphasis added). In St. Paul's day, both men and women typically wore long, loose garments that came down at least to their knees. Before undertaking any strenuous activity, the first thing they had to do was to gather up their loose clothing and tuck it into their girdle. Only after this were they free to undertake any vigorous action. We see the phrase "gird up your loins" several times. Using the girdle of truth means that we take seriously the admonition in Hebrews 12:1–2 to lay aside the sin that clings to us: "Therefore, since we are surrounded by so great a cloud of witnesses, let us also lay aside every weight and the sin that clings so closely, and let us run with perseverance the race that is set before us, looking to Jesus the pioneer and perfecter of our faith." If we do not "tuck them up" out of our way, those sins of habit will weaken us in the battle. In Psalm 51:6, David says, "Behold, you desire truth in the inward parts, and in the hidden part You will make me to know wisdom." God reveals his hidden wisdom only to those who have truth in their inner parts.

"*The breastplate of righteousness*" protects our *heart* (Eph 6:14, emphasis added). Proverbs 4:23 warns to "keep [guard] your heart

3. Prince, *Spiritual Warfare*, 1.
4. "Full Armor of God," http://www.christianarsenal.com/Christian_Arsenal/Full_Armor_of_God.html.

with all diligence, for out of it spring the issues of life." The Sermon on the Mount teaches us that the pure in heart shall see God. What are the attacks against the heart of man? They are threefold: to misuse sex, to live in pride, and to love money. These "heart conditions" allow the enemy of our souls to gain a foothold in our lives.

By putting on the breastplate of righteousness, I protect my heart, my desires, and my motivations. In my early days as a young Christian, my friends and I would ask the question, "Where is your heart?" By seeking first his kingdom and its righteousness, we put our hearts in the right place and are protected in these areas of our lives.[5]

"*The shoes of the preparation of the gospel of peace*" are the next piece of our armor (Eph 6:15, emphasis added). Roman legionaries were equipped with very sturdy sandals. The open design of *caligae* (their Roman name) allowed for the free passage of air to the feet and, unlike modern military boots, was specifically designed to reduce the likelihood of blisters forming during forced marches, as well as other disabling foot conditions like tinea or trench foot. Socks were not worn with caligae, although in colder climates such as Britain, woolen socks were used. Caligae were constructed from three leather layers: an outsole, the middle openwork layer which formed the boot's upper, and an insole. They were laced up the center of the foot and onto the top of the ankle. Additionally, iron hobnails were hammered into the soles to provide the caligae with reinforcement and traction and also an effective weapon against a fallen enemy. These made them highly mobile. They could make long forced marches at short notice.[6]

As Christians, we need to be *mobile*—available to God for his purposes wherever and whenever he calls upon us—even at short notice or in unexpected circumstances. Someone has said that God requires us to have one major ability for this kind of protection and movement—*availability*. To wear the boots of warfare, I present myself as a willing instrument for God's purposes daily.

5. Prince, "Because of the Angels," 2.
6. Prince, "Because of the Angels," 2.

I prepare myself to tell my story when the Lord opens the door of opportunity. I am not ashamed of the Gospel.

"The shield of faith" is our next piece of armor (Eph 6:16). The word here, translated "shield," relates to the word for a "door." Its length was greater than its width. A trained soldier could crouch down and draw his body in so that he was completely protected, but he had to be fit and athletic. An overweight man would not be fully protected. Our shield of faith must likewise cover our whole person. No aspect of our life can be withheld from the Lord. As we study Scripture and apply the teachings of the church, we will cover ourselves and our families with God's protection.

God has always promised his people covering and protection. However, to qualify for that protection and covering, we must do our part. The shield of faith means a total surrender to Jesus Christ and his ways. Anything in our lives that is superfluous or self-indulgent will be outside the protection of our shield.[7]

The arrows Satan uses against us are "fiery." A direct hit can cause destruction and death. They are designed not merely to wound but also to set on fire wherever they are aimed. Satan desires to "set on fire" my family, my means of income, my relationships, and my health. But the shield of faith—if used with diligence and persistence—will not merely stop the arrows, it will *quench* them. It will extinguish the flames![8]

"The helmet of salvation" protects our minds. Just as the breastplate protects our *heart*, so the helmet protects our thought life (Eph 6:17, emphasis added). The mind is the area in which Christians are regularly attacked. Inside our minds, there is often a continuing war. Satan seeks to insinuate thoughts that will disturb us or distract us or in some other way make us ineffective in our war against him. In 2 Corinthians 10:3–5, St. Paul teaches us: "Indeed, we live as human beings, but we do not wage war according to human standards; the weapons of our warfare are not merely human, but they have divine power to destroy strongholds. We destroy arguments and every proud obstacle raised up

7. Prince, "Because of the Angels," 2.
8. Prince, "Because of the Angels," 2.

against the knowledge of God, and we take every thought captive to obey Christ."[9]

Every Catholic should come to realize that meditating on Scripture and using disciplines like *Lectio Divina* has eternal consequences. It is much more than mere intellectual exercises. We are bombarded with thoughts, images, negativity, and lies. Pornography is a multi-billion-dollar industry that reaches the highest levels of spiritual leadership, including clergy and seminarians. This area itself needs serious attention from our bishops as countless Catholics, especially men, are held captive by this snare of the evil one.[10] Addictions, abortion, divorce, sexual predators, racism, and division plague our culture. A strategy of response from individual parishes is not optional. It is necessary! There is a battle raging! Putting on the helmet of salvation means guarding our thoughts from sunup to sundown!

At this point, St. Paul taught us that the armor is primarily for *protection* or *defense*. He then turned to weapons of *attack*. If we attempt to attack before we have secured our defense, we are unprepared for the enemy's counterattack, which is one main reason why many Catholics are wounded and become casualties. They try to attack without protection! We should now look to our *offensive weapons*. "*The sword of the Spirit*," which is the Word of God, is used both for attack and defense, but primarily for the assault (Eph 6:17).

It is said, "The best defense is a great offense." This is often true in the spiritual realm. The term here translated "word" is the Greek word *rhema*, which usually denotes an expression that is *spoken*. "Word" here does not refer to the big Catholic Bible sitting on the coffee table. Rather, it means taking the Scripture and voicing it, proclaiming it boldly, by which it becomes a sharp, two-edged sword.

Please note that it is "the sword of the [Holy] Spirit." We take the Scripture in our mouth, but it only becomes powerful when the Holy Spirit activates the word. As previously mentioned, the perfect pattern of how to use the sword of the Spirit is provided by the

9. Prince, "Because of the Angels," 2.

10. Carroll et al., "The Porn Gap."

encounter of Jesus with Satan at the time of his temptation in the wilderness. Three times Satan approached Jesus with a temptation, and each time, Jesus resisted the evil one with the same phrase: "It is written." Jesus used the *rhema*—the spoken word of the Lord. God has made this same approach available to each of us.[11]

Please remember two things. First, Jesus had already been "filled with the Holy Spirit." It was the Holy Spirit in Jesus that directed him in the use of the sword. Second, Jesus read, meditated, and knew the Scripture. When Satan confronted him, he did not need to go to someone else. He did not have to "find a Bible." He had deposited the sacred Scriptures in his heart. Surely, we today need to follow the Lord's example!

The last piece of armor and spiritual weapon is referred to as "*All prayer*" (Eph 6:18, emphasis added). This seventh weapon is not listed in the same way as the previous six, but it is needed to make the equipment of the Christian soldier complete. Of the previous six items, only the last one—*the sword of the Spirit*—is a weapon of attack, and even the sword is useful only for hand-to-hand combat. But this seventh weapon of *all prayer* expands the spiritual realm in which we can operate. We are no longer limited to our immediate surroundings. We can move anywhere the Spirit leads us. We are not controlled by geography and space. This powerful tool is available no matter what state we find ourselves in. We can be young, old, clergy, religious, laity, male, or female. The opportunity to affect history and change it for the purposes of God is available to all Catholics alike![12]

Similar to the sword, previously mentioned, this weapon of *all prayer* depends on the Holy Spirit for its effectiveness. It must be prayed "in the Spirit." God does not commit such a weapon to Christians who are guided only by their carnal desires, emotions, or idolatry. *All prayer* includes many kinds of prayer, such as those listed in 1 Timothy 2:1— supplications, prayers, intercessions, and giving of thanks. It is not a solo instrument to be played by one Christian on his own. Rather it is produced by an orchestra of

11. Prince, "Because of the Angels," 2.

12. Prince, "Because of the Angels," 2.

many instruments blended in harmony by the Holy Spirit. Sometimes it takes apparently insurmountable obstacles to provoke this kind of prayer.

In Acts 4:15–18, the Apostles were confronted with a satanic strategy that could have put a stop to all further evangelistic activity. The Jewish Council, which was the supreme religious authority of the Jewish people, officially commanded the Apostles "not to speak at all nor teach in the name of Jesus." The opponents of the Gospel were perceptive enough to recognize the unique importance of the name of Jesus. The entire effectiveness of the Gospel was dependent on it. As Peter himself had declared to the council: "Nor is there salvation in any other, for there is no other name under heaven given among men by which we must be saved." By this decree of the council, Satan had built a "stronghold" that would have prevented all further progress of the gospel or growth of the infant church.

Confronted with this satanic scheme, all the believers came together to seek God's help. Blended into an orchestra, they cried out to the Lord for his intervention. God responded with such a demonstration of his power that "the place where they were assembled together was shaken, and they were all filled with the Holy Spirit, and they spoke the word of God with boldness." The weapon of *all prayer* had demolished Satan's stronghold. In many parts of the world today, Satan has built up obstacles and opposition to the progress of the Gospel that resist all typical evangelistic methods. It is time for the church to deploy its most powerful weapon: the weapon of *all prayer.*

The battle for souls, families, nations, and the church itself can seem overwhelming to us. The evil one cannot be confronted and defeated through our own strengths and abilities. How then can we find confidence in this unseen warfare? The Good News of the Gospel is that Jesus Christ has defeated the devil, taken back the keys of death and hades Satan took in the garden, and destroyed him who had the power over death (Heb 2:14).

YOUR CHALLENGE

Commit to fast and pray on the first Friday of every month. From there, build fasting and prayer into a weekly, then a daily discipline. You must always combine your fasting with scripture and prayer.

> Fasting gives birth to prophets and strengthens the powerful; fasting makes lawgivers wise. Fasting is a good safeguard for the soul, a steadfast companion for the body, a weapon for the valiant, and a gymnasium for athletes. Fasting repels temptations, anoints unto piety; it is the comrade of watchfulness and the artificer of chastity. In war it fights bravely, in peace it teaches stillness.
> —St. Basil the Great[13]

---

13. Burghuis, "St. Basil the Great's First Homily on Fasting," 6.

Chapter 10

Encountering Jesus through Signs, Wonders, and Healing

[H]ow God anointed Jesus of Nazareth with the Holy Spirit
and with power; how he went about doing good and healing
all who were oppressed by the devil, for God was with him."

ACTS 10:38

ONE CANNOT READ THE Gospels, see the Gospel lived out in the
Acts of the Apostles, and/or read the writings of St. Paul without
concluding that signs and wonders were integral to the expecta-
tions of all who encountered the Lord. In fact, in the four Gospels, it was the power of God demonstrated through the Master
that brought people to attention and opened them to the message
(the raising of Lazarus was an amazing example of this). A culture of encounter will flourish and renew Catholicism as we not
only look for the supernatural signs to confirm an investigation
for the canonization of a saint, but as we also look for the signs of
God to spread and establish the truth of the Gospel! Today, in the
third millennium, encounters with Jesus that include signs, wonders, and healings are dynamics that a majority of Catholics have
neither considered nor sought. The purpose of this chapter is to

open our minds to the reality that Jesus desires, in the twenty-first century, to demonstrate his power within the Catholic Church.

For us to begin to rebuild this expectation and experience in our Catholic faith, we must first look at the early writings of the Apostolic and Church Fathers. We will discover that God's power surrounding the preaching of the Gospel (the *kerygma*) as well as the life of the church in community did not cease when the Apostles left the scene.

John 20:30 states that Jesus did "many other signs" that John was not able to include in his Gospel. He also records Jesus's promise to his disciples that the works that he did, they would also be able to do, and greater, because he was going to the Father (John 14:12).

As we survey the book of Acts and the New Testament letters, this is what we find. Acts 5:12 records, "Now many signs and wonders were done among the people by the hands of the Apostles." In 2 Corinthians 12:12, Paul tells the church, "The things that mark an Apostle—signs, wonders, and miracles—were done among you with great perseverance."

Generally speaking, "signs and wonders" refer to the most supernatural gifts of the Holy Spirit. It refers to healings, exorcisms, and knowledge and prophetic gifts. There is, of course, a large section of both the Catholic Church and Protestants which takes the view that these "signs and wonders" were given by the Spirit of God to reinforce the preaching and teaching of the Apostles. They were also the works provided to validate the words of the apostolic community who had seen the risen Christ, been commissioned by him, and given the unique enabling of the Holy Spirit to remember all that he had said and done. When, however, all the Apostles died, these gifts ended. Some argue this happened abruptly; others say that it was a gradual process over an extended period. It could compare to the progressive withdrawal of horse-drawn vehicles from the roads and their replacement by automobiles; in other words, it was a process that took one or two generations to complete. This disappearance of the gifts of the Holy Spirit, whether it is held to be sudden or gradual, is referred to as "Cessationism" or the "Cessationist" view. This view is taught in many Protestant settings. Catholics, on the other hand, have had a history of accepting the supernatural. They have, however, limited the extraordinary works of God and have rarely connected them to the typical Catholic Christian experience. Many Cessationists justify their opinion from 1 Corinthians 13:10, "When perfection comes, the imperfect disappears." The "perfection" which was to come is taken to be completion of the canon of the Scriptures and "the imperfect" which would disappear is the spiritual gifts about which Paul has been speaking in 1 Corinthians 12 and 13.[1] If the Cessationist view were correct, it would be the case that all the gifts of the Holy Spirit had ceased to function in the early church, at the very latest by AD 150. By that time, not only had the Apostles long since died, but most of those who had been taught by them had also died. There is plenty of evidence of the experience of baptism in the Holy Spirit and the use of spiritual gifts in the early Catholic Church right down to the great Ecumenical Church Council of 451 and beyond. We can examine some of the evidence that both baptism in the Holy Spirit and "signs and wonders" were clearly in evidence in the life and worship of the early Christian church during the first eight centuries.[2]

Justin Martyr (110–165) was born of pagan parents but converted to Christ when he was about thirty years of age. He taught students in several important cities in the Roman Empire including Ephesus and Rome itself, where he opened a Christian School. In his *Dialogue with Trypho*, he wrote about the gifts of the Spirit in the churches with which he was familiar. He noted that the gifts of the Holy Spirit, including exorcism, were widely in use: *"For one receives the spirit of understanding, another counsel, another of healing, another of strength, another of foreknowledge, another of teaching and another of the fear of God. The prophetic gifts remain with us to the present time. For some [believers] do certainly cast out devils, so that those who have thus been cleansed from evil spirits do frequently both believe and join the church. Others have knowledge of things to come; they see visions and utter prophetic expressions"*[3]

1. Pennington, "A Case for Cessationism," para. 8.

2. McDonnell and Montague, *Christian Initiation and Baptism*, 314.

3. Martyr, *Dialogue with Trypho*, 82.

Hilary (315–367) was a fourth-century bishop of Poitiers in Gaul. He describes the experience of being filled with God's Spirit. He writes: "We who have been reborn through the sacrament of baptism experience intense joy (*maximum gaudium*) when we feel within us the first stirring of the Holy Spirit."[4] This emphasis on experience is something that Hilary felt to be particularly important. In another piece of writing, he declared, "among us, there is no one who, from time to time does not feel the gift of the grace of the Spirit."[5] Elsewhere, Hilary mentions the gifts of the Holy Spirit that this experience opens. "We begin," he says, "to have insight into the mysteries of faith, we are able to prophesy and to speak with wisdom. We become steadfast in hope and receive the gifts of healing."[6] Hilary wrote these tracts near the end of his life around AD 360. It is evident his baptism and early experience of the filling of the Holy Spirit was still a major focal point of his faith. In the same piece, he goes on to underline the importance of fully using the gifts which the Lord gives us. "These gifts," he wrote, "enter us as gentle rain. Little by little they bear fruit."[7] Apparently, Hilary anticipated that healing, evangelism, and other gifts grew in Christian people as they developed the faith, and Hilary encouraged the faithful to reach out and use them. His advice, given in his *Tract on the Trinity* was, "Let us make use of such generous gifts."[8]

St. Cyril (315–387), who was bishop of Jerusalem in the later years of the fourth century, was an important leader in the Holy City and wrote a great deal, including some significant pieces on the Eucharist. He thought of the church in Jerusalem, as indeed all others, as standing in a succession of outpourings of the Holy Spirit, a history of the Spirit which connected to Moses. St. Cyril gave a series of twenty-three lectures to those who were preparing for baptism. In one of them, he stated that the Spirit is "a new kind of water" and that what the Spirit touches the Spirit changes. "Great,

4. Scotland, "Signs and Wonders."
5. Scotland, "Signs and Wonders."
6. Scotland, "Signs and Wonders."
7. Scotland, "Signs and Wonders."
8. Scotland, "Signs and Wonders."

omnipotent and admirable," he continued, "is the Holy Spirit in the gifts."[9] Although he wrote at a time just after Constantine had been converted to Christianity and the church was beginning to become more structured and institutional, he did not restrict the gifts to those who were ordained. He was adamant that "hermits, virgins, and all the laity have these gifts of the Spirit." Following the Apostle Paul in 1 Corinthians 14:3, Cyril urged the Christians in his pastoral care "to receive the gift of prophecy."[10] St. Cyril's last instruction to his baptismal candidates was "to prepare your souls for the reception of the heavenly gifts."[11]

Both St. Basil of Caesarea (330–379) and St. Gregory of Nazianzus (329–389), who were prominent bishops in Asia Minor, also expected that the miraculous would be initiated at the time when new Christians were baptized in water and hands were laid on them with a prayer for the reception of the Holy Spirit. St. Gregory of Nyssa (331–395), Basil's younger brother, wrote a biography of Gregory the Wonderworker, a third-century North African Christian. In chapter 77 he commented that one of Gregory's great marvels was that he accomplished his many healing miracles "without any special fuss."[12] In other words, it was not meant to bring attention to itself. Again, he wrote, "but for the deliverance from demons and the cure of bodily ills the breath from his mouth was sufficient."[13] In the following chapter, Gregory of Nyssa further commented, "To go through in order all the marvels worked by him would require a long book."[14]

The continuance of the gifts of the Holy Spirit within the early Catholic Church is evident. St. Patrick (385–451) was an example of signs and wonders operating in the early history of our church. He was an Englishman who was captured in a raid and taken to Ireland as a slave for six years. He then escaped to Gaul where he

9. Cyril, *The Catechetical Lectures*, 16:11.

10. Cyril, *The Catechetical Lectures*, 16:11.

11. Cyril, *The Catechetical Lectures*, 16:11.

12. Gregory, *Life and Works*, 77.

13. Gregory, *Life and Works*, 77.

14. Gregory, *Life and Works*, 77.

trained as a monk. He eventually returned to England and was
sent out to take the Gospel to Ireland. Toward the end of his life,
Patrick wrote his *Confession*. In it he says: "He who wants to can
laugh and jeer, but I shall not keep silent nor keep hidden the signs
and wonders which have been shown to me by the Lord before
they took place, as He knows all things before the world began."[15]
In the seventh century, Muirchu wrote a biography of St. Patrick.
According to him, the evangelist to the Irish raised a man from
the dead by the name of Macula, and within hours he was in good
shape.[16] On another occasion, Patrick brought a man called Dare
and his horse back to life by sprinkling holy water on them. As a
result of this miracle, Dare gave Patrick an area of land on which
the city of Armagh was later founded.[17] In another instance, St.
Patrick also cursed a field belonging to an evil man by the name of
Mudebrod. According to Muirchu, it was still sandy and infertile a
hundred years later.[18]

We can begin to ask ourselves, through these early events,
the question of the necessity of creating an openness to this kind
of spirituality and practice. There are many more examples that
might be told. That may indeed be a goal for further writings. For
now, however, can we begin to consider a culture of encounter
that seeks and demonstrates the present supernatural activity of
the Holy Spirit? Can we not learn from those already mentioned?
Thaumaturgus the Wonderworker, Hippolytus, Gregory Bishop
of Constantinople, St. John Chrysostom, and our beloved St. Augustine all testify to signs, wonders, and healings as part of their
Catholic experience.

I would be remiss if I did not include the fact that my family
has experienced God's signs, wonders, and healings throughout
our journey. Early on in our marriage, Leslie and I were devastat-
ed by the death of our first child, Andrea, born eight weeks premature. She lived for two days and then the Lord took her home

15. Scotland, "Signs and Wonders."
16. Patrick and Hood, *St Patrick: His Writings and Muirchu's Life*, section 23.
17. Patrick and Hood, *St Patrick: His Writings and Muirchu's Life*, section 25.
18. Patrick and Hood, *St Patrick: His Writings and Muirchu's Life*, section 25.

(a wonderful Catholic doctor baptized her in the ambulance as she was transferred to the Ohio State Medical Center). After our baby's death, Leslie learned from a specialist that she had a congenital uterine malformation and the possibility of never having a full-term pregnancy was something we needed to accept. While at our lowest point, a lay brother in a small-group setting had a prophetic word for us: "For surely, I know the plans I have for you, says the Lord, plans for your welfare and not for harm, to give you a future with hope" (Jer 29:11). When this word was spoken to us, it produced a supernatural hope and calm for the first time since our daughter had died. We had a renewed sense that God was with us! A few months later, "unplanned," Leslie was again pregnant. During her first trimester I was on a ministry trip in Ohio and just before I was scheduled to speak, Leslie called and was bleeding profusely. A friend was coming over to take her to the hospital. I went to a room and lay down, full of fear, anxiety, and doubt. All the past, painful feelings were rushing through me. Suddenly, it was as if the Spirit hovered over me and lifted an extreme weight. I had a clear sense that God was in some form of control, and I had a supernatural peace. I went on to the meeting and gave a talk. After the meeting, I immediately called home and discovered the baby's heartbeat had been strong and seemed to be firmly planted in the womb. Our son James was born on December 20 at the University of Kentucky Medical Center. He was five weeks premature but healthy and strong. We took him home at 5:00 a.m. Christmas day and put him under the Christmas tree! God was healing bodies and hearts that day! Leslie went on to carry three more of our children, and each of them were a full-term pregnancy and born after the due date. God had healed my wife's womb and our broken hearts.

I end this chapter with a scene from the book of Acts, the place I believe God is calling the church to renew her spirituality. The scene is a gathering in a group after Peter and John were arrested and brought before the council of the chief priests and elders. They had returned, and the church began to pray:

After they had been released, they went to their friends and reported what the chief priests and the elders had said to them. When they heard it, they raised their voices together to God and said, "Sovereign Lord, who made the heaven and the earth, the sea, and everything in them, it is you who said by the Holy Spirit through our ancestor David, your servant: 'Why did the Gentiles rage, and the peoples imagine vain things? The kings of the earth took their stand, and the rulers have gathered together against the Lord and against his Messiah.' For in this city, in fact, both Herod and Pontius Pilate, with the Gentiles and the peoples of Israel, gathered together against your holy servant Jesus, whom you anointed, to do whatever your hand and your plan had predestined to take place. And now, Lord, look at their threats, and *grant to your servants to speak your word with all boldness, while you stretch out your hand to heal, and signs and wonders are performed through the name of your holy servant Jesus."* When they had prayed, the place in which they were gathered together was shaken; and they were all filled with the Holy Spirit and spoke the word of God with boldness. (Acts 4:23–31, emphasis added)

Can we raise our voices to the Lord the same way our spiritual ancestors did?

YOUR CHALLENGE

Personally, and with others, begin to pray as the Apostles did in Acts 4. Ask the Lord to give us new boldness. Begin to pray for people who need a sign, wonder, miracle, or healing. When God does it, tell your story to others! The Word will spread!

Chapter 11

Encountering Jesus in the Call to Suffer for the Gospel

SINCE RETURNING TO THE Catholic faith, I have been reacquainted with the church's teaching and emphasis on redemptive suffering. St. Pope John Paul II wrote a most important document on the subject. He explored this theme in his Apostolic Letter *Salvifici Doloris*.[1] St. Pope John Paul II (né Karol Wojtyla) not only penned this document, his whole life became a model for suffering as a Christian. He was in third grade when his mother died; his only sibling, an older brother, died three years later; he discovered his father dead on the floor in their apartment. Karol Wojtyla was an orphan at twenty. His troubles were not limited to the loss of his entire family. The Nazis overran his country, and he did hard labor in a stone quarry. During the Nazi rule, many of his friends were killed, some in concentration camps, others shot by the Gestapo for the crime of studying for the priesthood. He himself was run down by a German truck and nearly died. When the Nazis finally left Poland, he and his countrymen came under the rule of the dictator Joseph Stalin. Later in life, his beloved church was torn apart by the storm that followed the Second Vatican Council. At

1. Kaczor, "A Pope's Answer."

sixty, an Islamic assassin shot him, and he nearly died again. As an old man, he suffered from debilitating Parkinson's disease that rendered him immobile, distorted his physical appearance, and finally took his ability to speak. Pope John Paul II knew about human suffering. His writing and his experiences are true gifts to the church and cause for our veneration. He is my patron saint and hero.

With all of this said, if indeed Catholicism in the West is to be renewed and reinvigorated, we must discover another suffering, one that we choose. I would call this suffering, *suffering for the Gospel*. Let me introduce this idea by examining the sacred Scriptures:

> Do not be ashamed, then, of the testimony about our Lord or of me his prisoner, but join with me in *suffering* for the gospel, relying on the power of God. (2 Tim 1:8, emphasis added)

> And for this reason, I *suffer* as I do. But I am not ashamed, for I know the one in whom I have put my trust, and I am sure that he is able to guard until that day what I have entrusted to him. (2 Tim 1:12, emphasis added)

> Share in *suffering* like a good soldier of Christ Jesus. (2 Timothy 2:3, emphasis added)

> For which I *suffer* hardship, even to the point of being chained like a criminal. But the word of God is not chained. (2 Tim 2:9, emphasis added)

> My persecutions, and my *suffering* the things that happened to me in Antioch, Iconium, and Lystra. What persecutions I endured! The Lord rescued me from all of them. (2 Tim 3:11, emphasis added)

> As for you, always be sober, endure *suffering*, do the work of an evangelist, carry out your ministry fully. (2 Tim 4:5, emphasis added)

I often refer to the Second Letter to Timothy as St. Paul's last will and testament. It was written around AD 67 during the Apostle's second imprisonment under Emperor Nero. The earliest persecution of Christians in Rome was so fierce that many of Paul's companions had deserted him (2 Tim 1:15, 4:10–11). St. Paul compared himself to a runner who was about to cross the finish line. He had reached the end of his apostolic mission and the wreath/crown awarded to the martyrs awaited him (2 Tim 4:6–8). Timothy had been the disciple of Paul for fifteen years and was summoned to receive the baton and continue to spread the Gospel. Paul later referred to this Gospel as *my gospel* (Rom 2:16, 16:25). As he awaited the beheading that would usher him into the presence of the one he loved, Paul called Timothy to embrace this Gospel and proclaim it accordingly.

Among the many exhortations to Timothy are the ones that say suffering is inevitable as the truth of the Gospel is proclaimed. Paul used his life and the endurance he modeled as a challenge to Timothy to do the same (2 Tim 3:10–14). Paul told Timothy the time would come when he too must pass the baton to his immediate successors but also to the future generations (2 Tim 2:2). If we are to accurately interpret St. Paul's writings, we must conclude that suffering for the Gospel is at the very heart of the apostolic faith passed on to the Christian generations. This mentality will call the church to a new boldness and a new understanding of our mission.

One half of the Acts of the Apostles is dedicated to the ministry of St. Paul. What do we conclude the Holy Spirit had in mind in recording all his adventures and sufferings for the one he served? Listen to the call Jesus gave him in the now famous encounter on the road to Damascus:

> Now there was a disciple in Damascus named Ananias. The Lord said to him in a vision, "Ananias." He answered, "Here I am, Lord." The Lord said to him, "Get up and go to the street called Straight, and at the house of Judas look for a man of Tarsus named Saul. At this moment he is praying, and he has seen in a vision a man named

Ananias come in and lay his hands on him so that he might regain his sight." But Ananias answered, "Lord, I have heard from many about this man, how much evil he has done to your saints in Jerusalem; and here he has authority from the chief priests to bind all who invoke your name." But the Lord said to him, "Go, for he is an instrument whom I have chosen to bring my name before Gentiles and kings and before the people of Israel; I myself will show him how much he must suffer for the sake of my name." (Acts 9:10–16)

We must conclude that St. Paul's call is not an anomaly. Rather, he is a model for the church to emulate as he often encourages us to do in his epistles. He sums up his sufferings in the Second Letter to the Corinthians.

But whatever anyone dares to boast of—I am speaking as a fool—I also dare to boast of that. Are they Hebrews? So am I. Are they Israelites? So am I. Are they descendants of Abraham? So am I. Are they ministers of Christ? I am talking like a madman—I am a better one: with far greater labors, far more imprisonments, with countless floggings, and often near death. Five times I have received from the Jews the forty lashes minus one. Three times I was beaten with rods. Once I received a stoning. Three times I was shipwrecked; for a night and a day I was adrift at sea; on frequent journeys, in danger from rivers, danger from bandits, danger from my own people, danger from Gentiles, danger in the city, danger in the wilderness, danger at sea, danger from false brothers and sisters; in toil and hardship, through many a sleepless night, hungry and thirsty, often without food, cold and naked. And, besides other things, I am under daily pressure because of my anxiety for all the churches. Who is weak, and I am not weak? Who is made to stumble, and I am not indignant? (2 Cor 11:21–29)

The list here is staggering. When used as an overlay for my own life and sacrifice for the Gospel, I am ashamed. St. Paul penned this letter around AD 56, eleven years before his martyrdom. He had more suffering ahead of him in those eleven years. Paul used his sufferings to legitimize his call and mission and to offer it as a strong contrast to his peers who boasted in a false apostleship. We must conclude that encountering Jesus Christ, spreading his Gospel, and being a witness for the name is a call to suffer. It is a call that we cannot escape, yet one we must choose to embrace. If the Gospel is to prevail in our personal lives and in the generation in which we live, we must take up this cross and follow him. Yes, it is a cross we choose to pick up! May the Lord give us the strength and courage to do so!

Many of my stories of suffering for the gospel, unfortunately, are from days past. In the early days of my work among college students, I would go the campus and share the faith. Sometimes I would go alone and other times I would be in a team. I noticed in the campus newspaper that a psychic was to be a keynote speaker during freshman orientation activities. He was to address the entire incoming class at the student union, with several thousand in attendance. I felt the Holy Spirit wanted me to attend the meeting, so I went and found a seat toward the front of the auditorium. During the entire presentation, as the psychic spoke, my spirit was agitated. I am reminded that Paul's spirit became provoked as he saw Athens full of idols. As the presentation came to an end, the psychic stated that the crowd should take a break and upon returning he would give practical tools on how to become more psychic. As he dismissed the crowd, I stood to my feet, and with a loud voice asked everyone to wait a moment. I proceeded to announce that the Scripture warns us about practicing the things the speaker addressed. I quoted Deuteronomy 18 which states that anyone who practices these occult and psychic deeds is an abomination to the Lord! With that, the psychic gave a retort, attacking me and the faith. With that the students went into the break. I sat in my seat praying and waiting. I had a clear sense of being filled with God's Spirit and encountering the boldness of Jesus Christ. At the end of the break, only a mere handful reappeared in the auditorium. From the several thousand in attendance, only a couple hundred returned. I got up and departed, knowing the Lord had used me to keep many from the psychic's grasp and Satan's oppressions.

St. Barnabas and St. Paul were on their first missionary journey in Acts 13–14. At the end of those chapters we find them exhorting the believers with some parting thoughts as they prepared to return to their base at Antioch. "After they had proclaimed the good news to that city and had made many disciples, they returned to Lystra, then on to Iconium and Antioch. There they strengthened the souls of the disciples and encouraged them to continue in the faith, saying, 'It is through many persecutions that we must enter the kingdom of God'" (Acts 14:21–22). This message was to the new believers. It was not given uniquely to clergy and the hierarchy.

I encourage my readers to reflect on the Acts of the Apostles. Allow it to be not just a story from the past that makes for interesting knowledge. Allow this sacred Scripture to form within you a spirituality that surrenders to the Lord in a whole new way. Allow it to cause you to volunteer for the Lord's purposes at this stage of your life.

It is never too late to respond to the Lord's call. I personally, as a Catholic Christian, believe that Jesus is asking me to re-up and be available to serve him. The time has ceased to be a casual Christian. The time is now!

YOUR CHALLENGE

Meditate on the Scriptures in this chapter. Pray for that apostolic boldness we see in the Acts of the Apostles. Begin to be on the alert to stand up for your faith and choose to suffer for it!

Chapter 12

Changing the Culture Means Changing the Narrative

WHEN WE HEAR THE call to change, all of us, by nature, have a negative response. I am reminded of when St. Peter sat on the rooftop of Simon the Tanner's house. He saw the sheet of unclean animals descend from heaven, and the Lord said to Peter, "Rise, kill and eat." The lead apostle, like the obedient subject that he was, immediately said, "By no means, Lord; for I have never eaten anything that is profane or unclean" (Acts 10:14). *This book is a call for change.* The change I am suggesting is one which challenges American Catholics to form a new culture which is an ancient one renewed by the Holy Spirit. This culture will be one that is known for its lifestyle of encounter with Jesus Christ, previewed for us in the Acts of the Apostles, and presented to us again by St. Pope John Paul II through his writings and apostolic mission. Someone once pointed out that most of the New Testament letters end with the word "amen." There is no "amen" at the end of Luke's writing of the Acts. Rather than an "amen," Luke and the Holy Spirit left us with a powerful image. The implication is that what St. Paul was doing must continue until the end of time. "He lived there two whole years at *his own expense* and *welcomed all* who came to him, *proclaiming the kingdom of God and teaching about the Lord Jesus*

Christ with all boldness and without hindrance" (Acts 28:30–31, emphasis added). I am moved by Luke's last words as he described the great Apostle fervently serving the Master. St. Paul sacrificed for the Gospel, using his resources to spread the Good News. He was a welcoming Christian who saw every person and situation as an opportunity. He saw the conditions of his life as divine appointments, orchestrated by the Holy Spirit, times for fellowship and conversion. He proclaimed the kingdom of God, that is the *kerygma*, and saw this proclamation as the gateway that must be entered to realize the kingdom. He also taught about Jesus Christ. This is the heart of the *didache*. If we preach and teach the church before the kingdom is proclaimed and Jesus Christ is presented in his fullness, we will continue to produce churchgoers and not disciples! St. Paul was bold! Simply stated, if the book of Acts is repeated in the church, there needs to be a call to boldness yet to be heard from the pulpits and ambos of the American Catholic Church. Finally, the Apostle had no hindrance. He prioritized his whole life around the Lord and his kingdom. He had possessions in proper perspective, and as he said in his writings, he learned the secret of prosperity and want. How can I change my life, so I too can reflect this kind of legacy if someone had to write a few sentences that summed up the activities of my life?

In Cardinal Timothy Dolan's blog post of July 13, 2016, we also hear him calling for the church to change.

> I don't think I'm breaking confidentiality here, but this was a frequent topic during the twelve day "congregation" of Cardinals between the resignation of Pope Benedict and the conclave that gave us Pope Francis. Cardinal after Cardinal challenged us that the most urgent pastoral need we have now is to renew the luster of the Church, to make it the light to the world and salt to the earth Jesus intends His body on earth to be, to revive it as the "universal sacrament of salvation" urged by Vatican II, to make her a bridge, not a fence, a magnet, not a repulsion, to reclaim the liberating unity of Christ and His Church.[1]

---

1. Dolan, "What God Has Joined Together."

Cardinal Dolan's post is a fantastic look into the fellowship that took place among the cardinals in preparation for electing Pope Francis. They were looking for renewal and restoration that would renew the *luster* of the church. The premise of this book is stated in these very phrases. To restore the luster of the church, I contend that luster is to be discovered and rediscovered in the Acts of the Apostles. There we can renew our spirituality and shed the secular clothing our culture strives to put on us. For instance, in Acts 2:40, St. Peter, as part of the *kerygma*, challenged the listeners to change their hearts and to change their culture: "And he testified with many other arguments and exhorted them, saying, 'Save yourselves from this corrupt generation.'"

As we find the luster the cardinals spoke of, we will find ourselves fully separating ourselves from the culture of death and destruction that surrounds us. You will be saving yourself from an ever increasing immoral and degrading society. "Sex with machines could become addictive, warns expert." How much more corrupt can the culture become?[2]

What, you may ask, are the touchstones of our corrupt generation? I would suggest four words that form the idolatry of the West and the American scene: *convenience, comfort, personal peace, and affluence.*

We must recognize and then separate ourselves from these four idols. I would suggest one create an internal filter system and ask the Holy Spirit to reveal areas of your life that are in union with these dynamics. I assure you, he will speak and help! To adequately respond to the *kerygma*, we must change our culture as well as our hearts!

As mentioned earlier in this book, the key to interpreting Acts and the key to creating a culture of encounter and the key to renewing the church is found in Acts 1:8. "But you will receive power when the Holy Spirit has come upon you; and you will be my witnesses in Jerusalem, in all Judea and Samaria, and to the ends of the earth." Acts is the lens we must look through to change the culture created through idolatry and secularization. In the context of this verse, the disciples had been asking him about "times and seasons."

2. Best, "Will Robots Be BETTER Lovers."

They wanted to know when the Lord would restore the kingdom to Israel. Rather than give hints to their eschatological curiosity, Jesus gave them their marching orders. He was very clear. Wait for the in-filling of the Holy Spirit. Then, be witnesses. This became the focus, which they obeyed, and encounter became the overarching result that emerged. Jesus built his church on this dynamic. This dynamic was meant to both sustain the church and, when necessary, renew the church. Church history testifies to this reality.

We are now coming to a crossroad. Our willingness to change what we say and what we do will require each of us to take stock of our spiritual condition. Clergy, religious, and laity will have to look in the mirror, as challenged in the book of James, and see what kind of people we have become. "But be doers of the word and not merely hearers who deceive themselves. For if any are hearers of the word and not doers, they are like those who look at themselves in a mirror; for they look at themselves and, on going away, immediately forget what they were like" (James 1:22–24).

In order to change the culture, each group in American Catholicism, clergy, laity, and religious, must change the narrative. Let me tell of a recent conversation that is an example of this need. A young woman was a candidate in the RCIA process and was preparing to become a Catholic Christian. A final step in her preparation to enter the church was to meet with the local parish priest, a deacon, and myself. We wanted to discuss with her what she had learned in the process and what concerns still were present as we looked to set a date for her entrance into the church. One of the experiences she spoke of was the change of attitude she was experiencing toward the nearby evangelical megachurch. This was the same megachurch I referenced earlier. At the Easter service, I had the distinct impression that the entire family sitting behind me were Catholics who were standing because Jesus was "meeting them" then and there. The young woman, who, by the way, had a clear conversion story, began to share how she no longer had the need to attend the megachurch as often as she had in the past. She told how the sense of worship originally experienced there was now being fulfilled in the Catholic context, particularly through the Eucharist. Father Joe (not his real name) is a young priest, ordained just five years ago in 2014. He is very engaging and zealous for the church. His office had all kinds of "cool stuff" spread around and made one think that this new generation of priests is much different than the generation of priests in my youth. He spoke with the woman as if he not only knew her background (she is twenty-three years old) but could relate very easily to where she came from in context, questions, and nuance. When she finished explaining her gradual exit from the evangelical megachurch, Father Joe went into an explanation saying that at least 40 percent of the people at this Christian community (he was careful not to call it a church, which according to Catholic documents, is precise) were probably baptized Catholics. He stated that the emotion, entertainment, and "pizazz" were all factors in drawing people to their services. The implication was that the people there were emotionally tied to the "pizazz" with the apparent delusions that resulted. This perception kept them from the actual fruit of their baptisms as practicing Catholics. At this point, I said, "Father, I believe the 40-percent figure is much higher. And, with all due respect, we are a major part of why those people are there and not here in the church." Fr. Joe nodded, but I am not sure he understood the implications of what I was saying. To repeat a major theme of this book: multitudes of baptized Catholics have never been addressed with the *kerygma* or proclamation of the gospel which requires a full-throated response to Jesus Christ.

The Church needs a reforming paradigm shift, especially in the West and especially in America. Paradigm shifts are not easy to make. "Since the 1960s, the concept of a paradigm shift has also been used in numerous non-scientific contexts to describe a profound change in a fundamental model or perception of events, even though Kuhn himself restricted the use of the term to the hard sciences."[3] The paradigm shift we all are familiar with took place in 1543: the transition in cosmology from a Ptolemaic cosmology to a Copernican one. I imagine myself in a small house in Italy in AD 1550. A neighbor knocks on the door. I open the door,

3. Lombrozo, "What Is a Paradigm Shift?"

and this neighbor friend of mine begins to tell me a story about a wide-eyed scientist who is starting to write about and speak about an idea that is just preposterous. He is teaching that the earth rotates around the sun! Ha ha! Who can imagine such foolery?

I conclude my thoughts by reflecting upon the Old Testament book, Joel. Of course, this is the Scripture from which St. Peter quoted on the Day of Pentecost. There is a three-fold theme in the book of Joel: desolation, restoration, and judgment. A quick reading of this short Scripture shows those three dynamics at work in the people of God. The Jews were decimated, and the country was ruined because of the disobedience of God's people. Fruitfulness ceased, and the fruit that remained was devoured. A call went out to all the lands to repent and pray, both priests and people. Because of the obedience to repent and pray, God promised the people of God he would restore them, which he did! Fruit-bearing and fruitfulness were restored to the Israelites! With this as a background, the Lord promised to pour out his Spirit on all of mankind. It is this portion of the Scripture that St. Peter quoted on the Day of Pentecost and proclaimed the *kerygma* to all who were listening (a text without a context is a pretext!).

The last chapter of Joel, which is a very short book that each of us should take the time to read to gain the full benefit of what God is saying to us, acknowledged that Israel and Judah are restored, but there is a coming judgment on those who do not heed the call to repent and pray. The Scripture ends with a picture of God's people in what is known as the Valley of Jehoshaphat (Joel 4:12). This is the place God sits and judges the nations. This valley is further described in verse 14 as a valley of decision: "Multitudes, multitudes, in the valley of decision! For the day of the Lord is near in the valley of decision." I am convinced that American Catholicism has been called to a *valley of decision*. We must decide if we will participate in the renewal of the church in our generation. As stated throughout this book, it will take humility, repentance, courage, and a bold mission all overseen by God's Holy Spirit! The result will be nothing less than the emergence of a new Catholic culture, a culture of encounter! God help us all, and may the transformation begin!

YOUR CHALLENGE

Psalm 110 verse 3 states that God's people will *"volunteer freely* in the day of Thy Power" (NASB, emphasis added). Get alone with the Lord and tell him you volunteer to become a disciple dedicated to an Acts of the Apostles spirituality!

Bibliography

Best, Shivali. "Will Robots Be BETTER Lovers than Humans? Sex with Machines Could Become Addictive, Warns Expert." http://www.dailymail. co.uk/sciencetech/article-3774191/Will-robots-BETTER-lovers-humans-Sex-machines-addictive-warns-expert.html#ixzz4JbV4KrVg.

Burghuis, Kent, trans. "St. Basil the Great's First Homily on Fasting." http:// rutgersnb.occministries.org/wp-content/uploads/2015/07/St.-Basil-the-Great%E2%80%99s-First-Homily-on-Fasting.pdf.

Carroll, Jason S., et al. "The Porn Gap: Differences in Men's and Women's Pornography Patterns in Couple Relationships." *Journal of Couple & Relationship Therapy* 16:2 (2017) 146–63.

The Catechism of the Catholic Church. Washington, DC: Office for Pub. and Promotion Services USCC, 1993.

"Changing Perspectives in Catholic Theology." http://www.ru.nl/ theology/@1037962/changing-perspectives-catholic-theology/.

Cyril. *The Catechetical Lectures of St. Cyril.* Oxford: Parker, 1845.

Doane, Peter. "A 'Convoluted' Pathway Home." http://chnetwork.org/2012/04/ a-convoluted-pathway-home-conversion-story-of-peter-doane/.

Dodd, C. H. *The Apostolic Preaching and Its Development: Three lectures, with an Appendix on Eschatology and Its History.* New York: Harper & Row, 1964.

Dolan, Timothy Cardinal. "What God Has Joined Together, Man Must Not Divide." http://cardinaldolan.org/index.php/what-god-has-joined-together-man-must-not-divide/.

Dunaway, Marc. *Building a Habit of Prayer.* Mt. Hermon, CA: Conciliar, 1989.

Gregory Thaumaturgus. *Life and Works.* Translated by Michael Slusser. The Fathers of the Church 98. Washington, DC: Catholic University of America Press, 1998.

Holy Bible: Catholic Edition. New Revised Standard Version. New York: Harper Catholic Bibles, 2007.

"The Jesus Revolution." *Time Magazine.* June 21, 1971.

John Paul, Pope, II. *Address to CELAM* (Opening Address of the 19th General Assembly of CELAM, 9 March 1983, Port-au Prince, Haiti). *L'Osservatore Romano* English Edition 16/780 (18 April 1983), no. 9.

————. *Apostolic Exhortation Ecclesia in America.* Vatican City: Vatican, 1999.

————. *Apostolic Letter Novo millennio ineunte.* Vatican City: Vatican, 2001.

————. *Encyclical Letter, Ecclesia de Eucharistia.* Vatican City: Libreria Editrice Vaticana, 2003.

————. *Encyclical Letter Redemptoris missio.* Boston: Pauline Books & Media, 1999.

————. "The Spirit of Truth." http://www.piercedhearts.org/jpii/general_audiences/gen_aud_1989/may_17_spirit_truth.htm.

Kaczor, Christopher. "A Pope's Answer to the Problem of Pain." https://www.catholic.com/magazine/print-edition/a-popes-answer-to-the-problem-of-pain.

Kerr, David. "Benedict XVI Tells New York Bishops to Speak Up for Truth." http://www.ncregister.com/daily-news/benedict-xvi-tells-new-york-bishops-to-speak-up-for-truth.

Lewis, C. S. *Mere Christianity.* New York: Touchstone, 1996.

————. *The Screwtape Letters; with Screwtape Proposes a Toast.* New York: Collier, 1982.

Lombrozo, Tania. "What Is a Paradigm Shift, Anyway?" https://www.npr.org/sections/13.7/2016/07/18/486487713/what-is-a-paradigm-shift-anyway.

Longenecker, Dwight. "Why Don't Catholics Read the Bible?" https://cruxnow.com/faith/2015/11/17/why-dont-catholics-read-the-bible/.

Martin, Ralph. "The Post-Christendom Sacramental Crisis: The Wisdom of Thomas Aquinas." *Nova et Vetera* 11.1 (2013) 57–75.

Martyr, Justin. *Dialogue with Trypho.* Selections from the Fathers of the Church 3. Translated by Thomas B. Falls. Edited by Michael Slusser. Washington, DC: Catholic University of America Press, 2012.

McDonnell, Kilian, and George T. Montague. *Christian Initiation and Baptism in the Holy Spirit: Evidence from the First Eight Centuries.* Collegeville, MN: Liturgical, 1990.

O'Leary, James. *The Most Ancient Lives of Saint Patrick: Including the Life by Jocelin, Hitherto Unpublished in America, and His Extant Writings.* New York: Kennedy, 2007.

O'Loughlin, Michael. "Pew survey: Percentage of US Catholics Drops and Catholicism is Losing Members Faster Than Any Denomination." https://cruxnow.com/church/2015/05/12/pew-survey-percentage-of-us-catholics-drops-and-catholicism-is-losing-members-faster-than-any-denomination/.

Paredes, Rebecca. "Here's What Porn Addiction Does to Your Brain—And How to Recover." https://www.bustle.com/articles/153055-heres-what-porn-addiction-does-to-your-brain-and-how-to-recover.

Patrick, Helgen, and A. B. E. Hood. *St. Patrick: His Writings and Muirchu's Life.* London: Phillimore, 1978.

Pelikan, Jaroslav, and Valerie R. Hotchkiss. *Creeds & Confessions of Faith in the Christian Tradition.* New Haven: Yale University Press, 2003.

Pennington, Tom. "A Case for Cessationism." https://www.gty.org/library/
sermons-library/TM13-7/a-case-for-cessationism-tom-pennington.

Pizzalato, Brian. "Suffering Can Lead to Salvation." https://www.
catholicnewsagency.com/resources/sacraments/anointing-of-the-sick/
suffering-can-lead-to-salvation.

"Pope Affirms 'Ignorance of Scripture Is Ignorance of Christ.'" https://zenit.org/
articles/pope-affirms-ignorance-of-scripture-is-ignorance-of-christ/.

Prince, Derek. "Because of the Angels: The Weapons of Our Warfare." http://
www.derekprince.org/Publisher/File.aspx?id=1000021500.

———. Spiritual Warfare. New Kensington, PA: Whitaker House, 2001.

Ratzinger, Joseph. The Legacy of John Paul II: Images and Memories. San
Francisco: Ignatius, 2005.

Roberts, Tom "The 'Had It' Catholics." https://www.ncronline.org/news/parish/
had-it-catholics.

Rotelle, John E., and Maria Boulding, eds. The Confessions. In The Works of St.
Augustine: A Translation for the 21st Century, Part I. Hyde Park, NY: New
City, 1997.

Schaff, Philip. History of the Christian Church. Vol. 3. Grand Rapids: Eerdmans,
1968.

Schaff, Philip, and Henry Wace, eds. A Select Library of the Nicene and Post-
Nicene Fathers of the Christian Church. Vol. 1. Grand Rapids: Eerdmans,
1979.

Scotland, Nigel. "Signs and Wonders in the Early Catholic Church 90–451 and
Their Implications for the Twenty-First Century." European Journal of
Theology 10.2 (2001) 155–67.

Sparks, Jack N. The Apostolic Fathers. Nashville: Nelson, 1982.

Thigpen, Thomas Paul. "Manual for Spiritual Warfare." Charlotte: TAN Books,
2015.

"This is a Prayer John Paul II Prayed Every Day." https://aleteia.org/2017/10/22/
this-is-a-prayer-john-paul-ii-prayed-every-day/.

Van Dam, Raymond. Saints and Their Miracles in Late Antique Gaul. Princeton:
Princeton University Press, 2011.

Weddell, Sherry A. Forming Intentional Disciples: The Path to Knowing and
Following Jesus. Huntington, IN: Our Sunday Visitor, 2012.

Wilson, Nate. "The Essentials of the Kerygma: What Must We Preach?" http://
www.natewilsonfamily.net/kerygma.html.